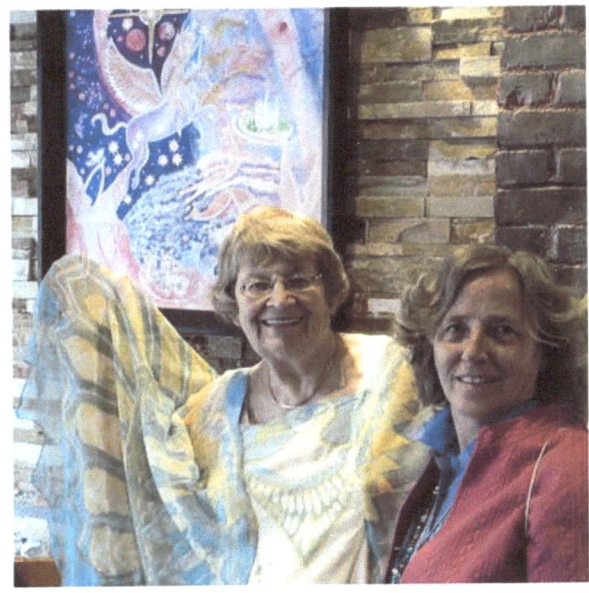

"Imagination Reigns"

"A book dedicated to the imagination and honoring the "Society for Art of Imagination" Preface, assembled, designed by Della Burford
Introduction by Brigid Marlin
The "History of the Society for Art of Imagination".
Copyright Brigid Marlin 2017

Artist bios by artists .. paintings
All rights for images and copyright belong to the respective artists. See index

ISBN 978-1-927825-04-4
Azatlan books
www.azatlan.com
contact dellaburford@hotmail.com
or azatlan@yahoo.com

"Imagination Reigns" in Ubud Bali
at Spirit of Writing and Art - Jan 27th - Feb 5th 2017 Opening 27th 4-8
Hosted by Della Burford/Norah Burford & Dale Bertrand
Show of the Members of the "Society for Art of Imagination"

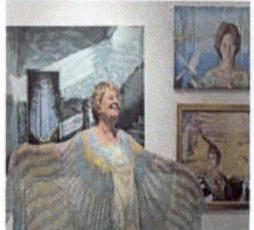 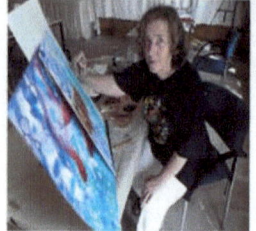 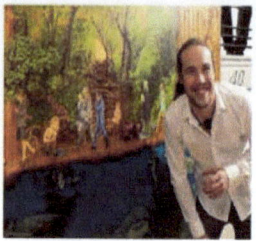 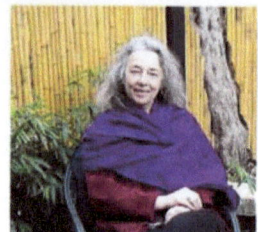

Brigid Marlin- Founder   Della Burford -Coord   Jean Pronovost   France Garrido

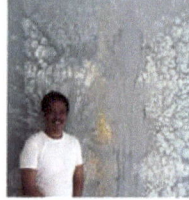 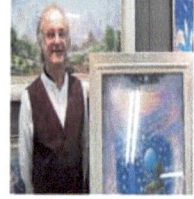 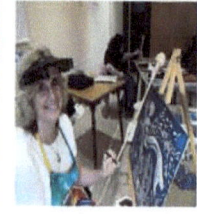 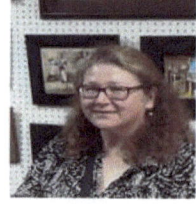 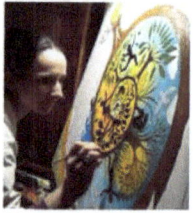 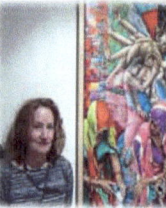

Wayan Karja Host in Bali   Benny Anderson   Cynthia Re Robbins   Debra Keirce   Gaia Orion   Kathleen Scarboro

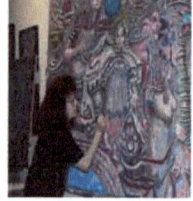 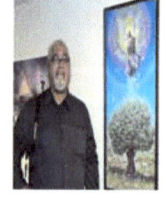 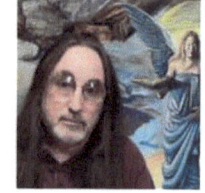 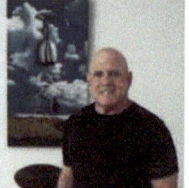 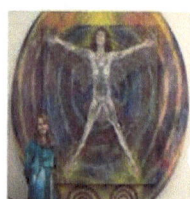 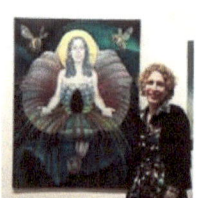

Olga Spiegel   Miguel Tio   Michael Coleman   William Otto   Irene Vincent   Liba W.S.

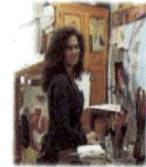 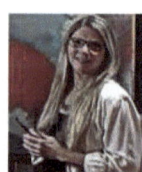 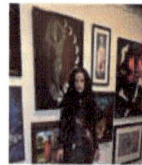 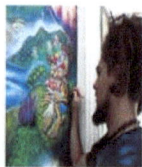 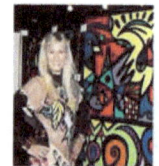 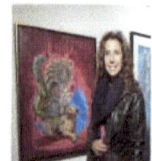 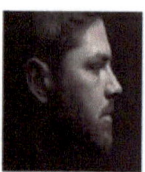

Lyne Lafontaine   Joanne St. Cyr   Rosemary Stehlik   Chris Dyer   Margot Bussiere   Heiidi Taillefer   Jerome Bertrand (former admid)

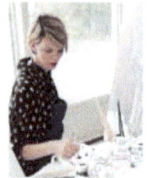 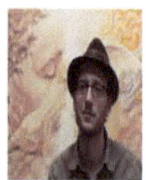 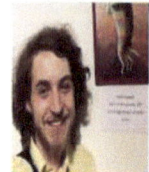 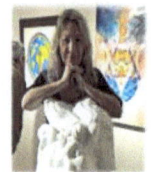 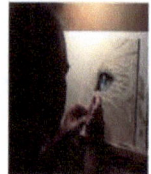 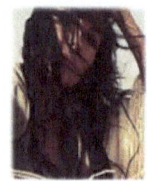 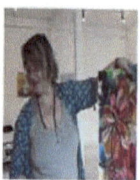

Georgina Smith   Dustyn Lucas   Ricky Schaede   Zeerka   Andrew Gonzalez   Fay Marineau   Sylke Gande

Index

1. Title Page
2. Poster for show - "imagination Reigns"
3. Index of Artists
4. Imagination Reigns Brigid & Della
5. Printer - Brad Grigor
6. Preface - Della Burford
7. Introduction - Brigid Marlin
   (History of Society for Art of Imagination)
   Artists featured (as they are on the Poster)
16. Brigid Marlin
17. Della Burford
18. Jean Pronovost
19. France Garrido
20. Wayan Karja (Host artist in Bali)
21. Benny Anderson
22. Cynthia Re Robbins
23. Debra Keirce
24. Gaia Orion
25. Kathleen Scarborough
26. Miguel Tio
27. Olga Spiegel
28. Michael Coleman
29. William Otto
30. Irene Vincent
31. Liba W.S.
32. Lyne Lafontaine
33. Joanne St. Cyr
34. Rosemary Stehlik
35. Chris Dyer
36. Margot Bussiere
37. Jerome Bertrand
38. Georgina Smith
39. Dustlyn Lucas
40. Ricky Schaede
41. Zeerka
42. Andrew Gonzalez
43. Fay Marineau
44. Sylke Gande
45 -57 Photos. Spirit of Writing and Art - Bali

"Imagination Reigns"

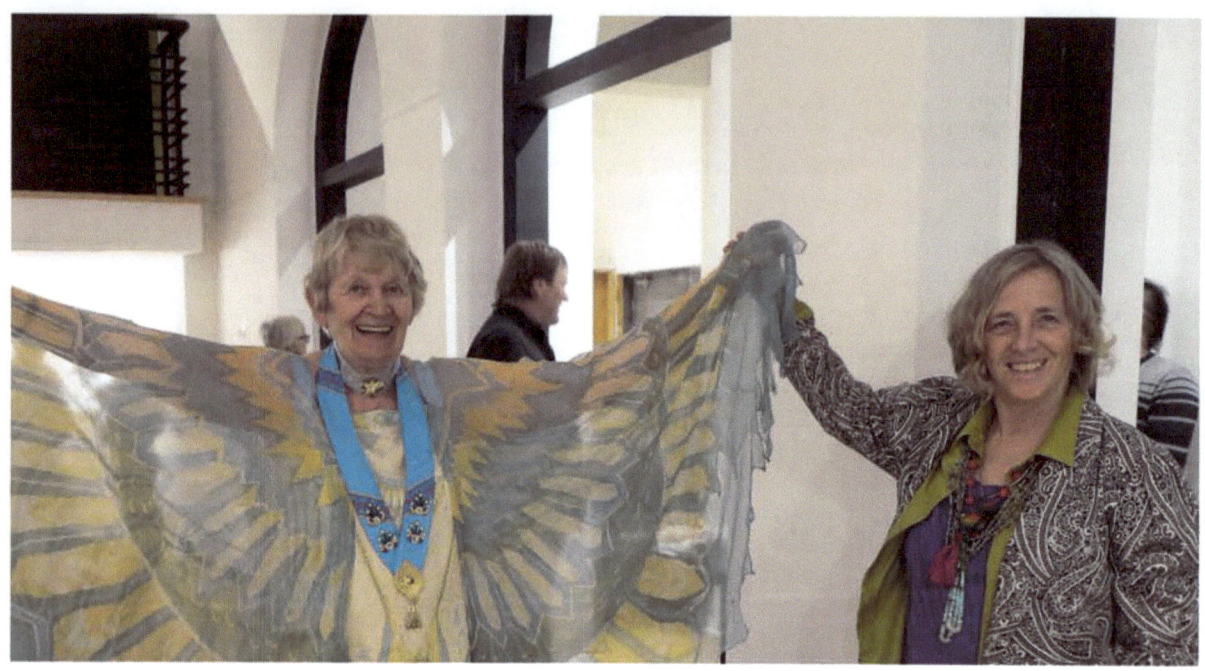

Brigid Marlin and Della Burford

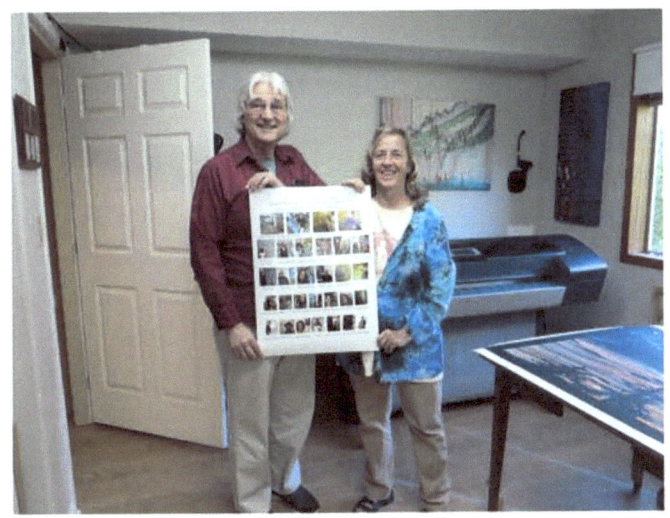

Brad Grigor at Turning Point Arts with Della holding Poster for the show in Bali.

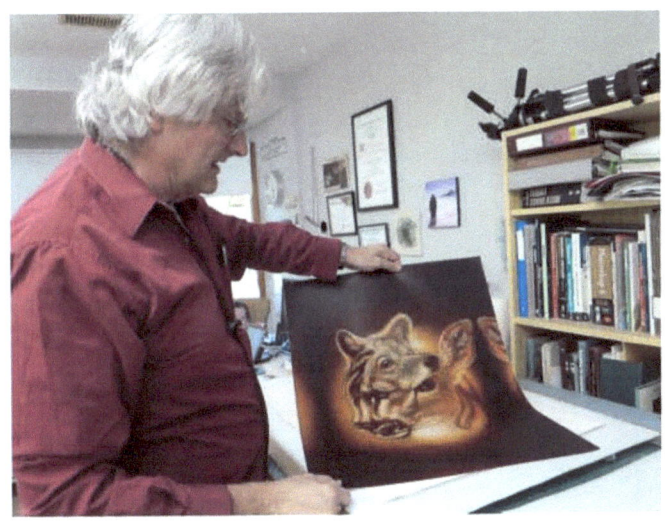

Brad Grigor with archival quality print that was done for the Bali show. It has a coating that will last 200 years. Some originals will also be shown in Imagination Reigns.

Preface for "Imagination Reigns" show/book by Della Burford

Turn up your imagination for a more enriched and inspired life!

All of the artist in the show/book show how their imaginations can create worlds. In selecting artist for this show/book I chose positive, life-affirming images. In painting them they are sharing visions, imagination and dreams.

In the front of the book is the introduction by the founder of the group - Brigid Marlin with a history of the Art of Imagination. I feel so honored to be share and assist her vision and goal of helping artist with imagination world-wide. At this time when our world has many crisis it is important to share positive visions so they can help people have a richer life by adding richness, we give strength and give life affirming energy. Our world is as rich as we want to make it and we do make the choice of image we want to have around us. This art in this book can bring happier and healing energy for ourselves and others.

I had the privilege of growing up with a mother who was an artist and also one with vision. Her main goal and one she shared with me as an important direction in my life was to be creative. I, because of her and other close friends support, including my husband Dale Bertand, was able to find my "bigger picture" and not only be creative but share it with the world. One of the stories/art in which I did this was "Journey to Dodoland" - "Where you can be what you want to be" and had the pleasure of seeing this dream shared internationally. As well as journeying and helping other journey to places of imagination I continued encouraging creativity in the "Magical Earth Secrets" and guide and directing it toward "making a difference" for the Planet Earth. My third book "Miracle Galaxy" I wrote and painted when in the process of self-healing from cancer. For this book I created imaginary angels to help me and others who were going thru a crisis. Imagination and dreams have been huge in my life and may be reason I am alive today. After completing a 40 year study of 2,000 lucid dreams I wrote my seventh book 'Dream Wheels' to encourage others to "live and manifest their dreams." So this is something dear to me and I am happy in this book to share other artist who are working from as the dream teacher Robert Moss would say "frontiers of consciousness".

"Imagination Reigns" book and show is acknowledging our creative potential and so "Imagination does indeed Reign". All of the artist who belong to the Society for Art of Imagination are so incredibly talented and have so much to offer the world - a few are shown here. I feel humbled to have a chance to share art from these artists. Most (20) I have met in person.

I would like to personally thank Brigid Marlin and all those who have been part and will be in the future artists of this illustrious organization - the Society of Art for Imagination. It is so enriching for humanity.

Thank you so much for all of your contribution! Please share!

HISTORY of Art of Imagination by Brigid Marlin
(written for her forthcoming book on Ernst Fuchs)
Copyright Brigid Marlin 2017

I. Art of Imagination through the History of Western Art II. Modernism and Its Unexpected Consequences 1910- 1990

The Origin and History of The Society for Art of Imagination

I. Art of Imagination through the History of Western Art. Art of Imagination is two-fold. It is the "art" – the skill and techniques evolved over centuries – and the "imagination" by which we mean the vision of the artist which lifts the work of art above the ordinary, and gives it a life of its own. This combination of art and vision has been created through time and blossomed at different periods throughout the history of art, notably in these periods:

14th -15th Century: The Early Flemish School which reached its high point in the visionary paintings of Jan van Eyck (1385-1441) and his brother Hubert who were the first to invent oil painting, Hieronymus Bosch (c1450-1516) painted visions which were full of a dark and surreal power.

15th Century: The Italian Renaissance produced the poetic paintings of Sandro Botticelli (c1444- 1510); the mystical beauty of the works of Piero della Francesca (c1415 -1492) and the powerful and enigmatic works of Leonardo da Vinci (1452-1519).

16th- 17th Century: The Flemish and Dutch Schools gave rise to Pieter Breughel the Elder (1525-1569) who gave a broad allegorical meaning to his landscapes, and Rembrandt van Rijn (1606-1669), who did paintings of great religious intensity.

18th Century: The English Mystic Artists were William Blake (1757- 1827) a poet and visionary only appreciated by a small circle of artists late in his lifetime, and his follower and admirer Samuel Palmer (1805-1881) who founded a school of artists based on Blake called the Ancients.

19th Century: The Pre-Raphaelite Brethren formed themselves in England to return to the sincerity of the Early Renaissance before Raphael developed his "grand" manner. The three most prominent members were

Sir John Everett Millais (1829-1896), William Holman Hunt (1827-1910) and Dante Gabriel Rossetti.

(1828-1892)

19th to early 20th Century: The Symbolists in France explored the exotic world of dreams. Begun by Gustave Moreau (1826- 1898) the movement embraced Odilon Redon (1840-1916) and Paul Gauguin (1848-1903). Other artists in the Symbolist school were Norwegian Edvard Munch (1863-1944), and Austrian Gustav Klimt (1862- 1918).

1924 -1945 The Surrealist Movement

was created after the first World War by artists and writers who were influenced by the horrors of the war and by their interest in the writings of Sigmund Freud. They were introspective, interested in exploring the subconscious. The most notable were Max Ernst (1891-1976), founder of Dada, Giorgio de Chirico (1888-1974), and Rene Magritte (1898-1967). Salvador Dali (1904-1989), with his dark dream paintings, became the most famous. In the USA Georgia O'Keeffe (1887- 1986) painted with a mystical intensity that was to influence many younger painters in America. O'Keeffe (1887- 1986) painted with a mystical intensity that was to influence many younger painters in America.

1945 – The Vienna School of Fantastic Realism

was formed after the Second World War when a group of young artists banded together. They were Erich Brauer, Ernst Fuchs, Rudolf Hausner, Wolfgang Hutter and Anton Lehmden, all marked by the horrors of the recent war. The founder of the group was Ernst Fuchs (1930 –2015) whose work reflected the terrible experiences of life in a Concentration Camp. After the war ended Ernst attended the Vienna Academy of Art and there discovered that techniques were no longer being taught. He journeyed to Paris and there began his research and experimentation which resulted in his rediscovery of the Mische Technique, one of the secrets of the Renaissance; a way of painting with egg-tempera and oil glazes which made the picture absolutely permanent. After an Exhibition of his work in this technique in Paris in 1954, Ernst Fuchs' fame spread abroad, and young artists from all over the world came to learn this technique, which he generously shared with all those who could learn from him.

A few years later many artists from America came to study with Fuchs. Bob Venosa (who taught mische with Martina Hoffman for 17 years from the 90's) Mati Klarwein, Phil Jacobson (who gives classes in mische today), Joseph Askew, Brigid Marlin (who gives classe in mische today), Herbert Ossberger, Linda Gardner, Clayton Campbell, Hanna Kay, Sandra Reamer and Olga Speigel, among others. They were joined by artists from as far away as Japan and Israel, and a new World-wide Art Movement was formed.

II. Modernism and Its Unexpected Consequences 1910- 1990

In the beginning of the 20th Century, art as it had been known began to change. The ever-increasing use of the photograph made mere copying obsolete. The Impressionists wished to make a new form of art by seeing the world anew and wonderfully fresh, but by its nature this fresh vision could not last, and they in turn were successively followed by Cubism and the Abstractionism. Artists, influenced both by disaffection with a world at war, and influenced by the growing interest in psychiatry became inward-looking, exploring their inner worlds, and experiencing a growing alienation from society.
The cult of the individual became supreme. Instead of Schools of Art giving rise to, and developing new talent, the concept came in of every artist as a lone genius.

This was reinforced in the Thirties and Forties by the Western artists' reaction to the heavy posterish images of the State Art in Nazi Germany, Fascist Italy and Communist-ruled countries. In contrast to this kind of didactic art, freedom to express oneself seemed the only important thing.

Yet now in the new Millenium there is a growing doubt as to whether this individualism has been carried too far. Has something been lost in the rush for absolute freedom?
In our day the new artists are seeking media attention by clever innovation, by "found objects" and by installing anything from dead animals to dirty furniture as exhibits. Perhaps now it is the artist as artist that is the real exhibit. The human ego writ large has replaced the former great asperations of art.

In a more idealistic age John Ruskin (1819- 1900) wrote, "What we want art to do for us is to stay what is fleeting, and to enlighten what is incomprehensible, to incorporate the things that have no measure, and immortalise the things that have no duration."

One unexpected consequence of Modernism is that the spiritual and universal quality of art has been lost.

With the lack of a common aim, the sense of a brotherhood among professional artists has disappeared. Perhaps each artist is trying to find an individual answer to the question "What is Art?". At the very dawn of Modernism the writer, Leo Tolstoy (1828- 1910) wrote, "We must distinguish art from counterfeit art. A real work of art destroys the separation between himself and the artist, and even between himself and all those others who also appreciate this art.

"[But now..] Instead of art which feeds the spirit, an empty and often vicious art is set up, which hides from us our need for true art. And true art for our time would demand the union of all people without exception — above all virtues it sets brotherly love to all men."

Another unexpected consequence of Modernism is that respect for the craft of art has diminished.

Many art schools are no longer teaching either drawing or the craft and techniques of painting and sculpture. Talented young artists are driven to despair as they find no real instruction is given to them, and no respect is accorded to the methods developed over time.

If action is not taken, the skills that have taken centuries to evolve will in due course disappear completely!

III. The Origin and History of The Society for Art of Imagination

In 1961 a group of artists from England, dissatisfied with the way the art world was going, began to work together, calling themselves the Inscape Group. They were Diana Hesketh (1931-), Peter Holland, .Brigid Marlin (1936-) Jack Ray and Steve Snell (1946-). They worked together to experiment with different ideas and techniques. Their progress may be summarised as follows:

1966 One member of the Inscape group, Brigid Marlin, went to study with Ernst Fuchs in Vienna. She was able to learn the Mische Technique, which was received with enthusiasm by other members who began to work with, and teach the technique in England, Europe and America.

1968 Members of the Inscape group were invited by Ernst Fuchs to come to Wartholz Castle, to his Summer Seminar, where artists from all over the world came to exchange ideas, and work together experimenting with old and newly evolved techniques. The Summer Seminar continued for seven years under the direction of Wolfgang Manner, and brought about great art and great friendships.

1972 As artists from different countries worked to promote each other and the cause of fine art, World-wide Exchange Exhibitions were set up in different countries and the Inscape Group became known as Inscape International.

1973- 1992 Inscape International. went on to exhibit in Paris, Ireland, Holland, Sweden, Tokyo, the United States and Canada. Lectures and classes were given on the Mische technique in Europe, the United States and Canada,

1993 Professor Ernst Fuchs summoned some of the Inscape artists to meet at Grafenegg Castle near Vienna to discuss the way forward towards promoting the Art of Imagination. He asked each artist to work towards this end. He had by now founded The Ernst Fuchs Museum in the villa built by Otto Wagner, and was planning an International Museum for Fantastic Art at the Saxe-Coburg Palais in Vienna.

1994 Maurizio Albarelli launched a major Exhibition "Du Fantastique au Visionnaire", the largest of its kind ever to be staged, at the Zitelle Cultural Centre, Venice, which included the work of many members of Inscape International. Robert Venosa was teaching mische with Martina Hoffman for 18 years in America.

1996 Rosemary Bassi organized the first of several shows of Fantastic paintings and sculpture including Inscape International Members at her Galerie Rolandseck near Bonn, Germany

1997 Inscape International decided to expand their Membership and work to help to promotion of Imaginative Art around the World. To facilitate this it changed its name to The Society for Art of Imagination. Ernst Fuchs agreed to be Honorary President.

1998 The Society for Art of Imagination launched a World Premiere- the very first Open Exhibition for Art of Imagination. It took place at the Mall Galleries, London. Virginia Rogers, a patron of vision, pledged to the Society $10,000.00 every year to distribute as prize money.

1999 The Erlangen Museum near Nurnberg, Germany, arranged a huge exhibition "Phantastik am Ende der Zeit" planned by Dr. Christine Ivanovic. The show was arranged in historical order, starting with the early woodcuts and engravings of Schongauer 1481, and Altdorfer c 1511, then on to the paintings of Bosch and Breughel, followed by Ensor and Munch, Max Ernst, Dali, and Paul Wunderlich. The Vienna School of Fantastic Realism was well represented, and the Exhibition displayed the work of many Members of The Society for Art of Imagination. The Exhibition formed part of a Symposium on Fantastic Art and attracted more than 10,000 visitors.

1999 & 2000 The Open Exhibition for Art of Imagination at the Mall Galleries continued. This Exhibition had now become a very popular annual event, giving artists of Imagination a public forum, and a chance to win valuable prizes. Many artists have been discovered through showing there, and have been taken up by visiting art dealers. The money awards helped artists who were finding it hard to survive.
A Magazine called Inscape was launched by the Society, to appear twice annually.
Lectures and classes were set up to spread the knowledge of good techniques in painting and sculpture.

2001: H.R. Giger agreed to become an honorary patron and invited Von Stropp, 1st prize winner of the 2000 exhibition, and other members of the Society to visit his home in Switzerland before travelling to the H.R. Giger Museum in Gruyere.
Damian Michaels, Australian member of the Society and editor of the acclaimed publication Art Visionary, mounted an exhibition of his international collection of fantastic and visionary art at the Orange Museum which was opened by Brigid Marlin on behalf of the Society.
The American Society for Art of Imagination was founded as a charity in Chicago through the inspiration and vision of Virginia Rogers. Ann Oestreicher based in New York became a generous patron with her donations for the next few years. The team working in the U.S.A. is France Garrido, Miguel Tio and Olga Spiegel.

A website featuring the works of the members was launched by Cynthia Re Robbin.
The annual exhibition was held in Cork Street, London before transferring to the Goldmark Gallery, Uppingham. England.
Michel de Saint Ouen succeeded Helen as editor of INSCAPE.
The annual exhibition was held in Cork Street, London before transferring to the Goldmark Gallery, Uppingham. England.
Michel de Saint Ouen succeeded Helen Cockburn as editor of INSCAPE.

2002: The annual exhibition was again held in Cork Street, London while an exhibition on the theme The Element of Water was displayed at the Mariners Gallery, St Ives, Cornwall. Art of Imagination, an exhibition of selected members of the Society was shown at the Obsidian Art Gallery, Stoke Mandeville, England. A show of African artists and international artists is at the Narobi Museum.

2003/2004: A travelling exhibition by members of the Society began at the Gallery in Cork Street, London before travelling to Kircudbright, Scotland and then forming the nucleus of the largest exhibition of imaginative art in the world at the Williamsburgh Art and museum, New York. The Society's works travelled to Miami.
Michel de Saint Ouen succeeded Brigid Marlin as Chairman of the Society.

2005: The Element of Water theme was repeated for an exhibition of the Society at Lauderdale House, London to celebrate UNESCO's year of water. The Inner Eye a European tour exhibition curated by Annabella Claudia Hoffman visited three countries. Myth and Magic, an exhibition featuring members of the Society was held at the Obsidian Art Gallery, Stoke Mandeville, England. A grand festival of the imaginative arts was held to celebrate the 10th anniversary of the Society at Lauderdale House, London. The festival included painting and sculpture, drama, writing, music and crafts.

2006: The Giger Museum, in Gruyeres, Switzerland hosted a month-long exhibition by the Society in the summer which was opened by the great man.

2007: The 12th Annual Exhibition held at the Mall Galleries, London, was opened by Sylvia Sims, a famous English actress. It was a great success and drew many visitors. Also that summer the Pennsylvania Institute of Science and technology gave us an Exhibition entitled "Where Science meets Art."

2008: The Society was invited to Shanghai to take part in a huge festival called Art Intrude. Artists were tasked to create art from everyday objects. Our Society chose to turn everyday umbrellas into exciting artworks. They were so successful that they went on to show in Italy, Nairobi, Kenya, and USA. We also helped fund art studies for children in Kenya.

2009: An Exhibition at the InterArt Gallery, New York; entitled Carnival of Venice, featured selected works by the Society's artists. The Society took part in an exhibition in Wessobrun, Germany. Saeby's Museum of Imagination brought the Society's artists' works to the attention of the citizen of Denmark.

2010: Fifty Years Fantastic, an exhibition celebrating works from the Society from its first beginnings in 1960 was held at La Galleria Gallery in the Royal Arcade, London. This 50th years exhibition was opened by Mary O'Hara. After closing it travelled to the Murphy Hill Gallery, Chicago as Five Decades of Fantastic.

2011: This year's annual exhibition was held at the Brick Lane Gallery, London. Being adjacent to the City of London's financial district it brought us a new audience.

2012: The Phantasten Museum was opened in Vienna in 2011 and the Society was invited to exhibit. Many of us travelled for the opening, celebrating the first ever Fantastic Museum for Imaginative Art. The Exhibition was opened by Professor Ernst Fuchs, who said he was delighted with the show.

2013: We returned to La Galleria, in the Royal Arcade, London, for our annual exhibition which was opened by internationally famous harpist David Watkins, who played one of his compositions on the Harp to the delight of the crowded rooms.

2014: This year our efforts switched to the American continent and the Canadian Society for Art of Imagination was launched with an exhibition in the prestigious Moniker Gallery in Toronto. Art for Peace featured over 50 International artists, and was curated by Marina Malvada and Bhatboy, who also curated a second series of exhibitions in Ottawa.

2015: Jean Pronovost, newly elected Chairman of the Canadian branch, curated an exhibition at the Ecomusee du fie Monde Montreal. It was very well attended and a great success. He also held an exhibition with the School of Fine Art in Cuzco, Peru.

2016: In the Spring we had a Paris exhibition, organized by Liba Stambollion; an exhibition in Seattle, USA organized by Don Farrell at the Krab Jab Gallery. There was also a huge Exhibition in the Park Gallery near Dresden, Germany.

2017 In early 2017 there was a show in Bali organized by Della Burford. Also a book published called "Imagination Reigns" featuring 30 Society artists who showed in Bali designed by Della Burford with an introduction of the History of the Society by Brigid Marlin. This year will also be a Society Exhibition at the One Art Space Gallery in New York in April/May.

"Imagination is more important than knowledge. Knowledge is limited - magination circles the globe." Albert Eistein

Brigid Marlin

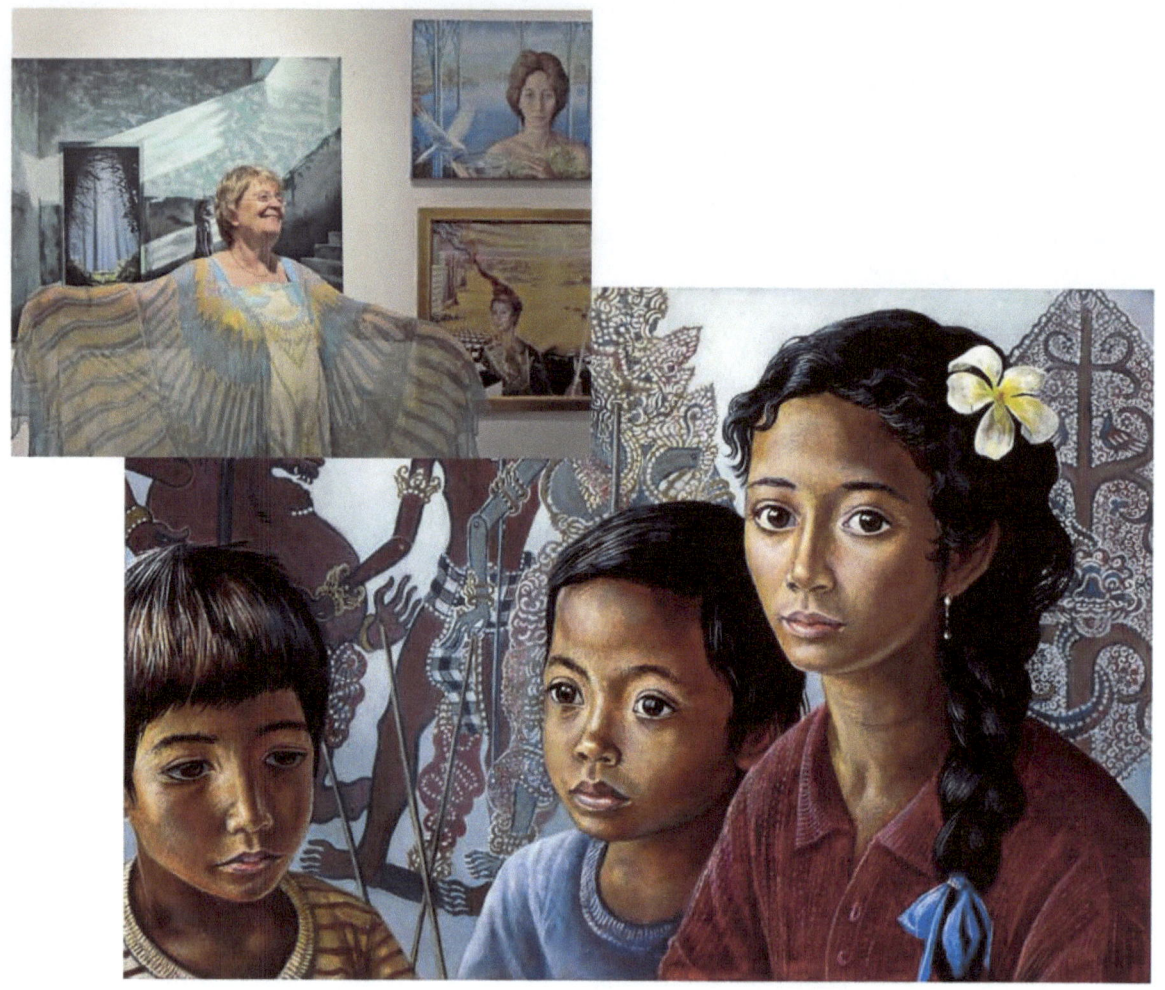

Brigid in 1998 founded the Art of Imagination to promote Visionary and and Fantastic Art World-wide. She was born in Washington D.C. She lives and works in Hertfortshire England.
She has exhibited her work all over the world and was part of the Arts Festival in Dubai in 2001. Among the portraits she has painted are the Dalai Lama, Queen Mother, Gertrude Crain of Crains, Communications, and Princess Mata-aho of Tonga. Her portrait of J.G.Ballard hangs in the National Portrait Gallery, and her portrait of Cecil Lewis founder of the B.B.C. hangs in Bush House. Her work is in the collection of Presidant Nixon, Lord and Lady William Butlan, Stanley and Christiane Kubrick and Virginia Roberts of Chicago.

" Imagination is one of the most important resources, using our unique expression it can guide us "

Della Burford

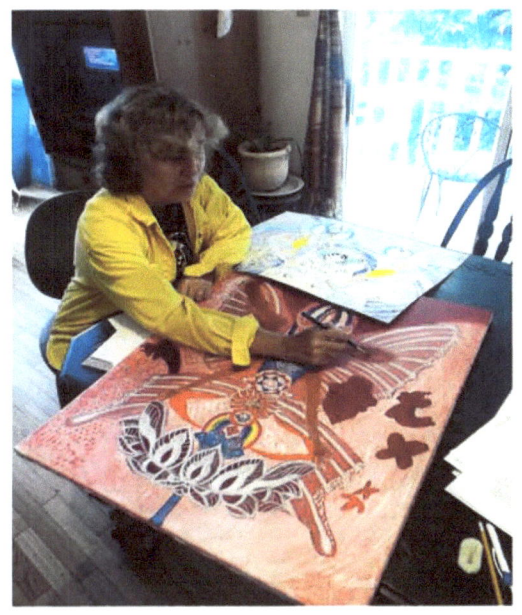
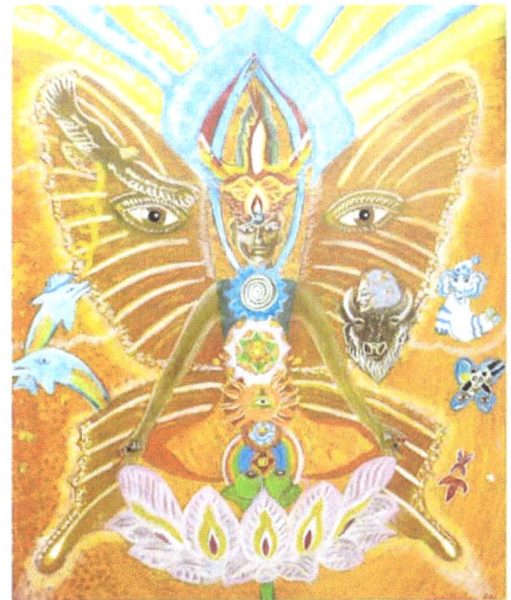

Della's paintings are inspired by dreams, different cultures, shamanism and imagination. She was born into art as her mother was a painter. She is a former teacher of Design at Humber College. She led art workshops for 20 years with the Inner City Angels. She also toured with her work to Mexico, Gautemala, Korea, North America and Bali. She painted large canvases for performances of her story at Museum of Natural History, B.A.M., Citycorp, 3rd Street Music School and the Smithsonian Institute. Her stories/art have been shared in Prisons, Hospitals and Cancer Centres. Her first book was gifted to 6,000 needy children. "Journey to a Lotus" was painted while travelling to India "Magical Earth Secrets" has been performed for four years in Japan by 100 % Parade. She has had two shows in Bali .. one of Dream Wheels and another of Dream Keys. After having a dream of Ernst Fuchs she decided to learn the mische technique and then completed "Dream Wheels" a book in which she shows how over 40 years she has manifested her dreams into art, writing and theatre for the World, Humanity and Spirit.

"Imagination is not the icing on the cake of life but the oven in which it is baked." Orna Ross

Jean Pronovost

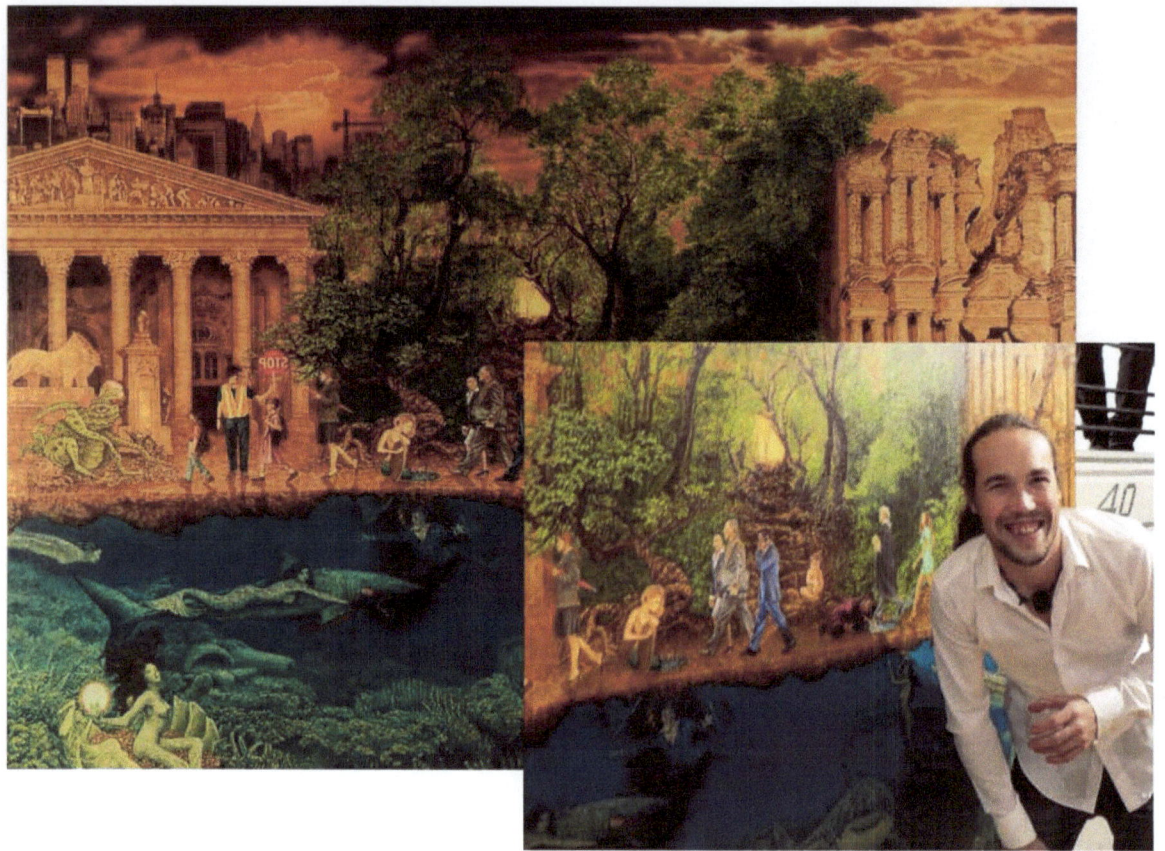

Jean Pronovost's art is not decorative-it is not abstract nor simply figurative but his art is visionary and allegorical. His creations are like opening books and leading us into a universe where the strange and mystical are kings. With the whip of a paintbrush, he carries us to the heart of an Inca legend or in the urban jungle. With a strike of a spatula, he reanimates a God faded from our memories or questions our humdrum. With striking realism, his paintings and sculptures unveil a world where yesterday signs can interact with our modern world. Fascinated with history and mythology, but also inspired by the magic of symbolism, Jean Pronovost uses archetypes rooted in ancient civilisations. Elegy of the essential and critic of all false values, the work of Jean opens the door of an alternative universe. In the world where we feel submerged by technological tools, where the conscience lose its way towards the quest of material gain, where the meaning of our life decays inside a society praising individualism and the power struggles, this artist questions our origins and offers his own personal vision of the world.

Imagination happens when I/We are open to the flow of and spark of spirit. When attuned to its organic ebb and flow, we are able to 'see' the light and dark and not be afraid of what it brings." France Garrido

France Garrido

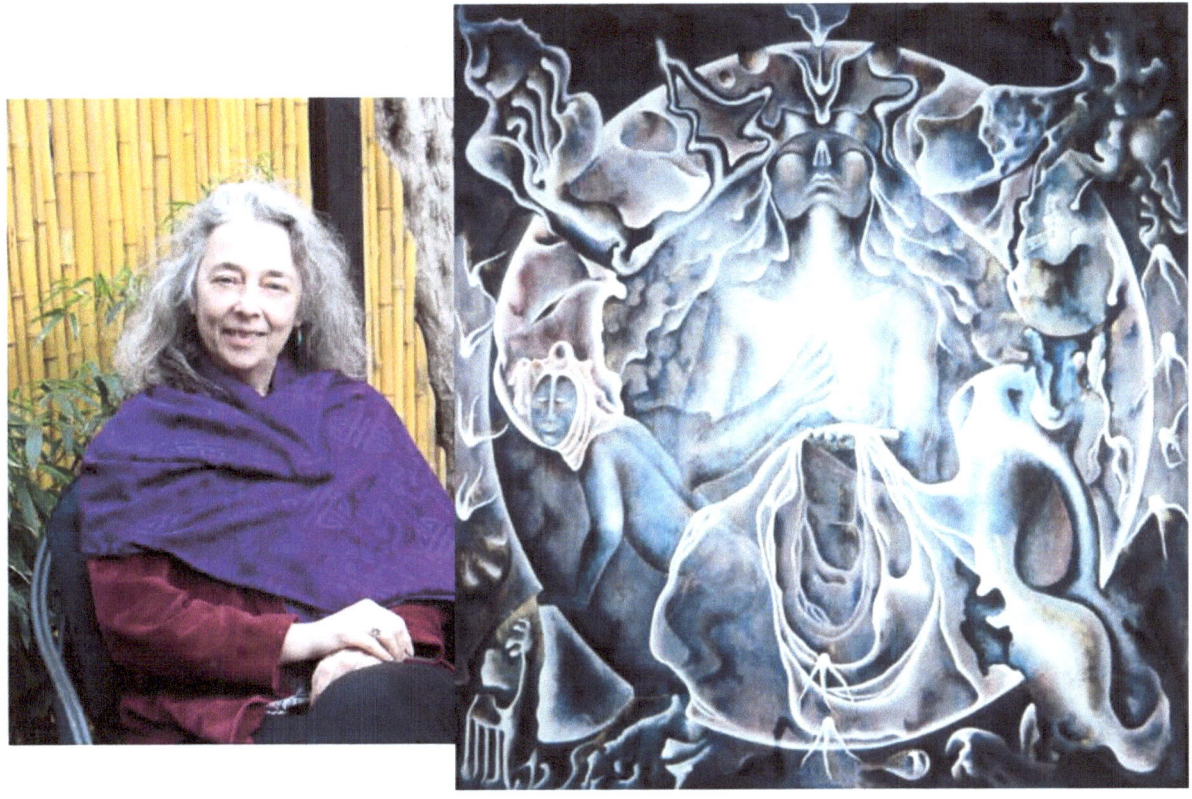

France Garrido likes to entice one into another world .. A world of vision and dream. She was born in New York City, N.Y. Her primary medium is collage/mixed media and secondary medium is acrylic paint. She has been greatly influenced by Hannah Hoch, Salvadore Dali, Dorothea, Tanning, Remedios Varo, Jorge Gonzalez Camarena, and many others as well as 'primitive cultures' worldwide. There have been other influences in her life, which have inspired her artistic growth. Nature and Spirit are key to that growth. Now she is focusing her attention on collage/mixed media, which has limitless fascination for her. Garrido works on an intuitive level, and allows the piece to speak and guide her during the process. These creations provoke a sense of mystery and spirit."I am seeking to touch; deep within the viewers spirit a truth or essence. To awaken/nudge/shift the unconscious."

"Follow your bliss and doors will open where there was no doors before."   Joseph Campbell

Wayan Karja (Host artist)

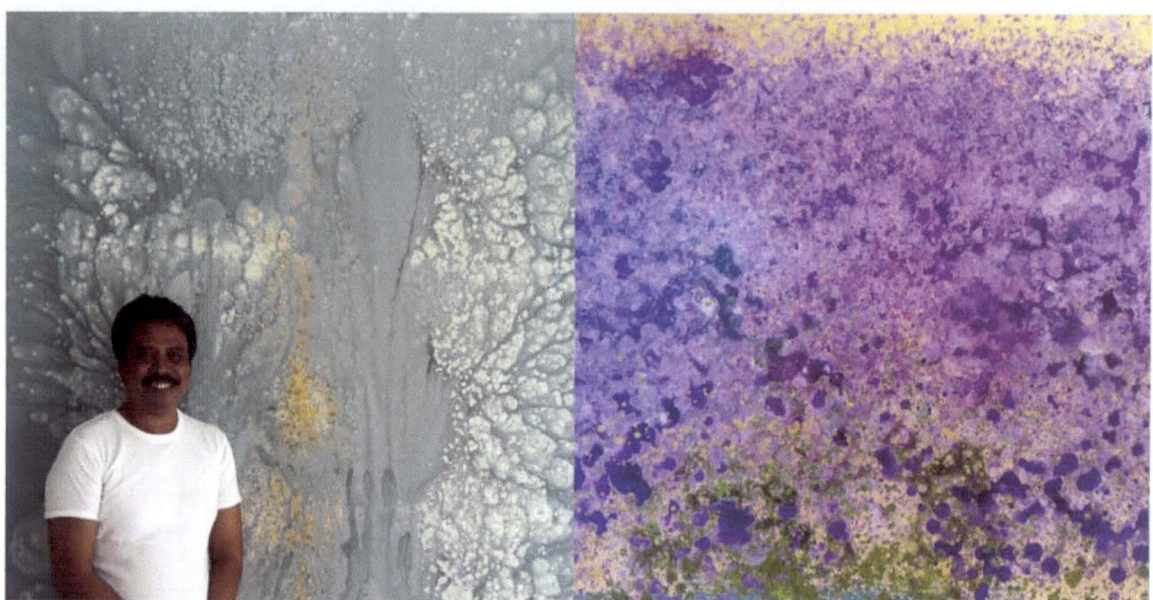

Balinese abstract artist Karja was born in a family of artists, his first memory is sitting on his father's lap with a brush in his hand. Karja leaned about colors as a young child from his father , His father, I Ketut Santra, introduced him to painting and then taught him the techniques. His father was one of the "Young Artists" of Penestanen inspired by Arie Smit who was a master of color. Karja studied three years of expressive art at the European Graduate School in Saas-Fee, Switzerland in 2008-2011, and this brought Karja to a new understanding of painting. He became the Dean of Fine Arts in Denpansaur University in 2014 but in the last while both teaches and works as an artists exhibiting in many international locations. Wayan for three years has taken part in the Spirit of Writing and Art program and the program is hosted at his villa Santra Putra. Last year he helped mentor various artists in the program. Wayan Karja finds solace in expressive art, as it liberates him from unnecessary attachments and allows him to find the therapeutic quality of art.

"She was richer in her dreams than realities : for things seen pass away and but the things unseen are eternal"
M.L. Montgomery - 'Anne of the Island'

Benny Anderson

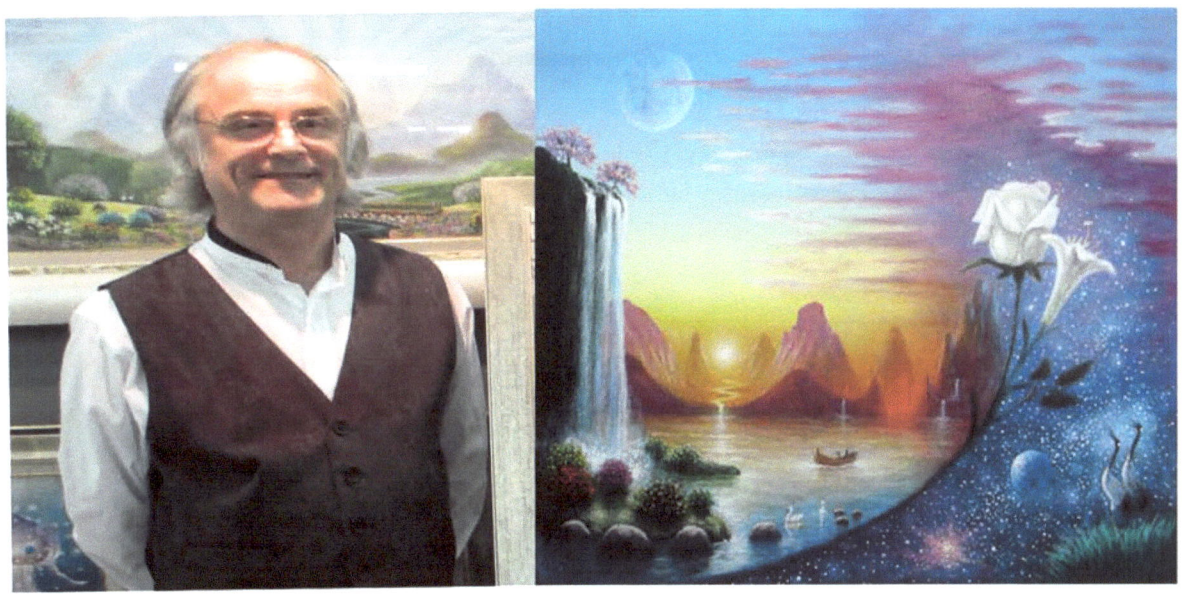

Benny explores realms of light and color in his art. He was born in Sweden in 1953.

Benny explores realms of light and color on his canvas. He was born in Sweden 1953. He studied art in Stockholm 1974 – 1977 and moved to USA in 1980. He has worked full time as artist since 1983. Benny lives close to New York City with his wife and 3 daughters. Inspiration for his art is a combination of great artists in the past and the inner visions I see today. Each painting is sometimes like a soul searching journey in itself. He feels it is a great moment when art can serve as an inspiration for viewers to find and release their own hopes and dreams

"The tree which moves some to tears of joy is in the eyes of others is only a green thing.. some scarcily see nature at all. But to the eyes of a man of imagination, nature is imagination itself"   William Blake

Cynthia Re Robbins

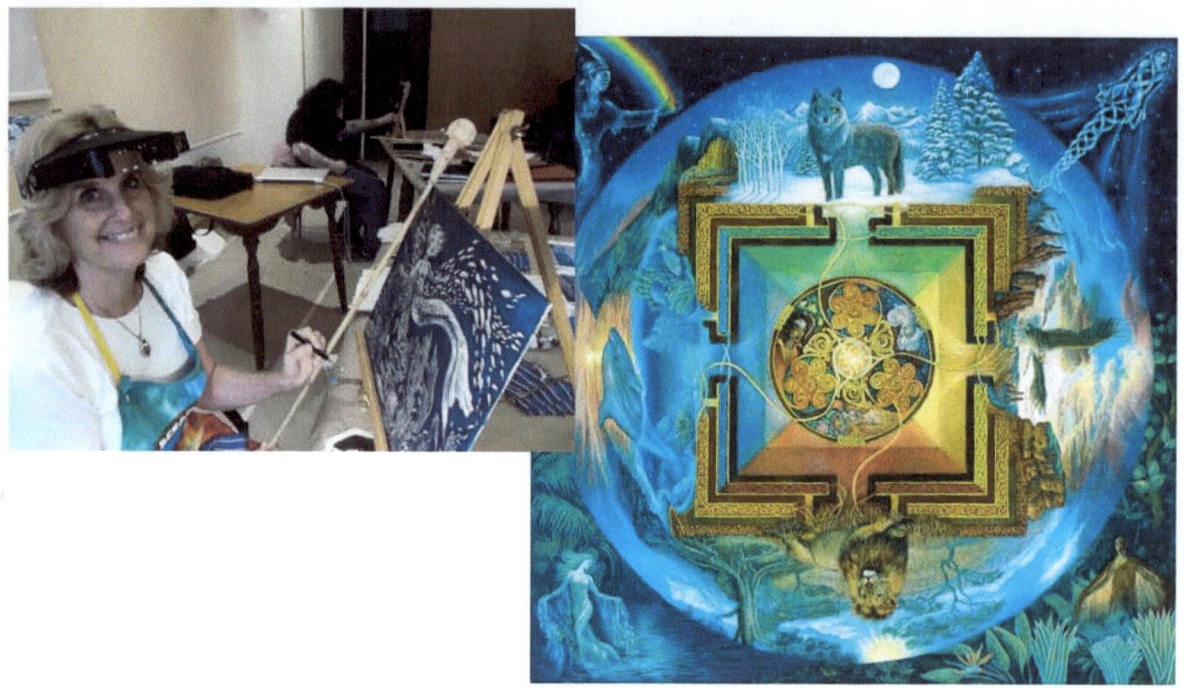

Cynthia studied at the Cleveland Institute of Art and Instituto Allende in Mexico, earning a BFA degree - major in painting. For 20 years she freelanced and lived in the Caribbean, while developing her personal style of painting. A pivotal year was 1993, in Boulder, Colorado when she studied with Robert Venosa, learning a transformational painting method, allowing for more perfection and an ethereal luminosity. Cynthia furthered her studies with Prof. Phil Jacobson, who teaches the traditional Mische technique, as it was taught to him by Ernst Fuchs. Cynthia continued her studies with Jacobson, Michael Fuchs, and Brigid Marlin. After another "tropical stretch", Cynthia now lives in Arkansas, surrounded by the ancient hills of the Ozarks. She is embarking on opening her own gallery in the historic downtown district of Eureka Springs, Arkansas. "The subject matter of my paintings has shifted along with life's passages and change of living environment, enriching my life and my art. Now I am focusing on what gives me the greatest joy. If my art makes us smile, I am achieving my goal."

"All things are possible until they are proven impossible."
Pearl. S. Buck

Debra Keirce

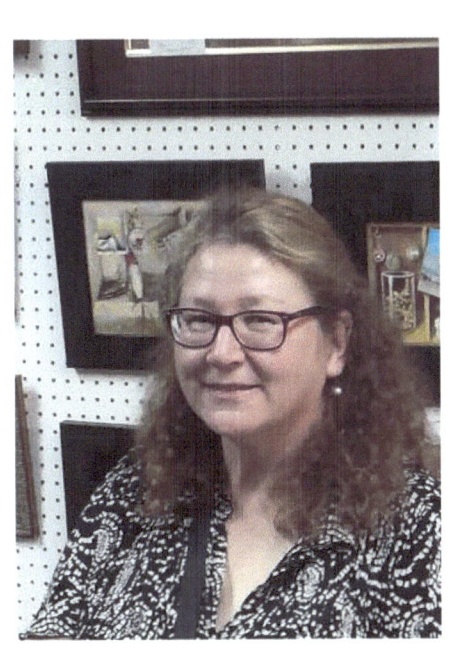
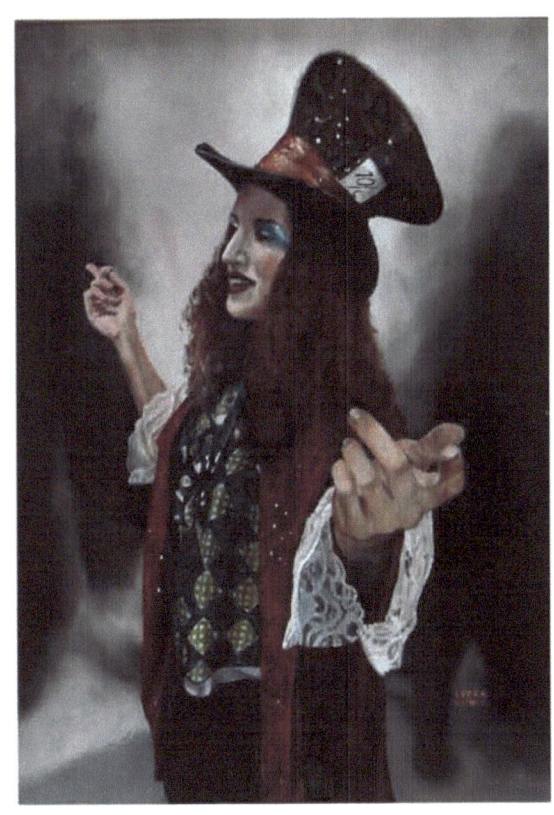

Debra creates paintings that tell stories of joy, desire, challenge and encouragement.
She considers the magic in our reality, and depicts it to the best of her ability. Using oil or acrylic paints, she draws from her own life to create art experiences for viewers across the globe. She paints in a tightly rendered realistic style with contemporary, Trompe L'Oeil and classical influences. She specializes in small paintings. Part of my process for creating miniature fine art involves the use of magnifying lenses and close range binoculars. She enjoys demonstrating these techniques for art lovers. Originally from Detroit, she has a degree in biochemical engineering and worked as a corporate engineer at pharmaceutical facilities for fifteen years. In 2010, she was able to begin painting full time. In December 2012 she was offered representation at Huckleberry Fine Art Gallery in Rockville, MD and Seaside Art Gallery in Nags Head, NC. In October 2014, Ellis-Nicholson Gallery asked her to become one of their artists.

" There are painters who transform the sun to a yellow spot, but there are others who with the help of their art and their intelligence, transform a yeallow spot into the sun." Pablo Picasso

Gaia Orion

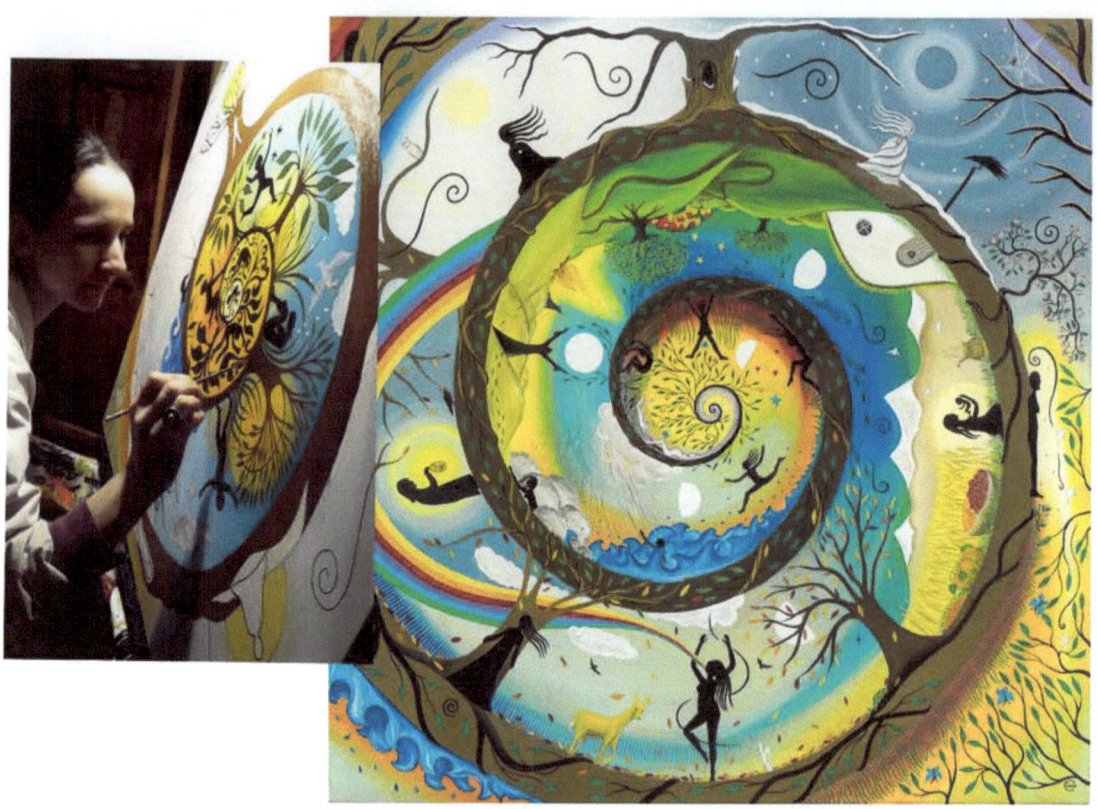

Gaia Orion has gained international recognition by participating in many worldwide projects that are working toward constructive world change. She has exhibited in Spain, Germany, Hungary, Mexico, the U.S.A and Canada with a recent solo show in Paris, France. In sharing the artwork and connecting with others she discovered that these transformational themes are part of a larger visionary movement that is active in society today... as deep ecology, social justice, conscious politic, alternative economy, and so on... Uniting our vision and natural talents can become a catalyst for individual and collective change so that we can move together toward a healthier humanity. Gaia originally hails from Paris, France, where she graduated with honours as an architect from Ecole des Beaux Arts in 1997. With her creativity she has found her way of sharing and connecting deeply with people.

"Imagination is a force of nature. Is this not enough to make a person full of ecstasy? Imagination, imagination, imgination. It converts to actual, it sustains, it alters, it redeems! Saul Bellow Henderson The Rain King.

Kathleen Scarboro

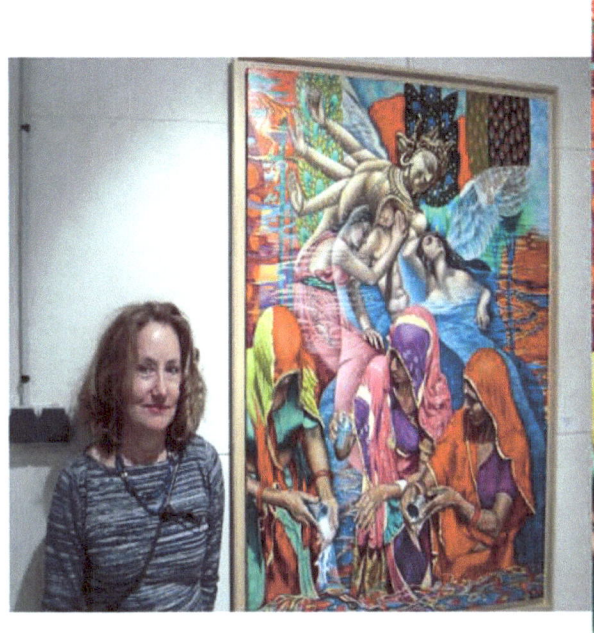
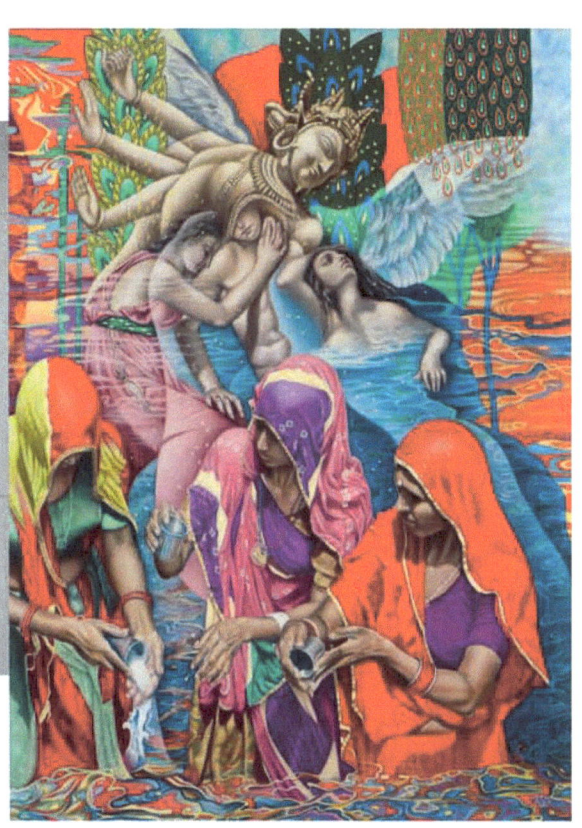

Kathleen likes to take the audience on an inner and outer voyage in her imaginative realism work.
Stylistically speaking, these works would fall into the category of magic realism or imaginative realism. She believes we are living in exciting times, and searching for meaning in a world that is in total transformation. She tries to express this constant metamorphosis of our view of reality in her paintings. Mystery lurks everywhere underneath a seemingly banal reality. It is this mystery that she pursues. she finds India is an amazing country, and she has taken on the challenge of attempting to express some aspects of its elegance and complexity. The paintings are executed in oil on linen canvas, in a technique which can be considereda contemporary version of the procedure used during the Flemish Renaissance by painters such as Jan van Ecyk and Rogier Van derWeyden. Paintings done in this labor intensive fashion require months of work; an average length of time for a medium size work being 2 or 3 months.

"If you change your imagination, you can change your mood." Stephanie Conkle

Olga Spiegel

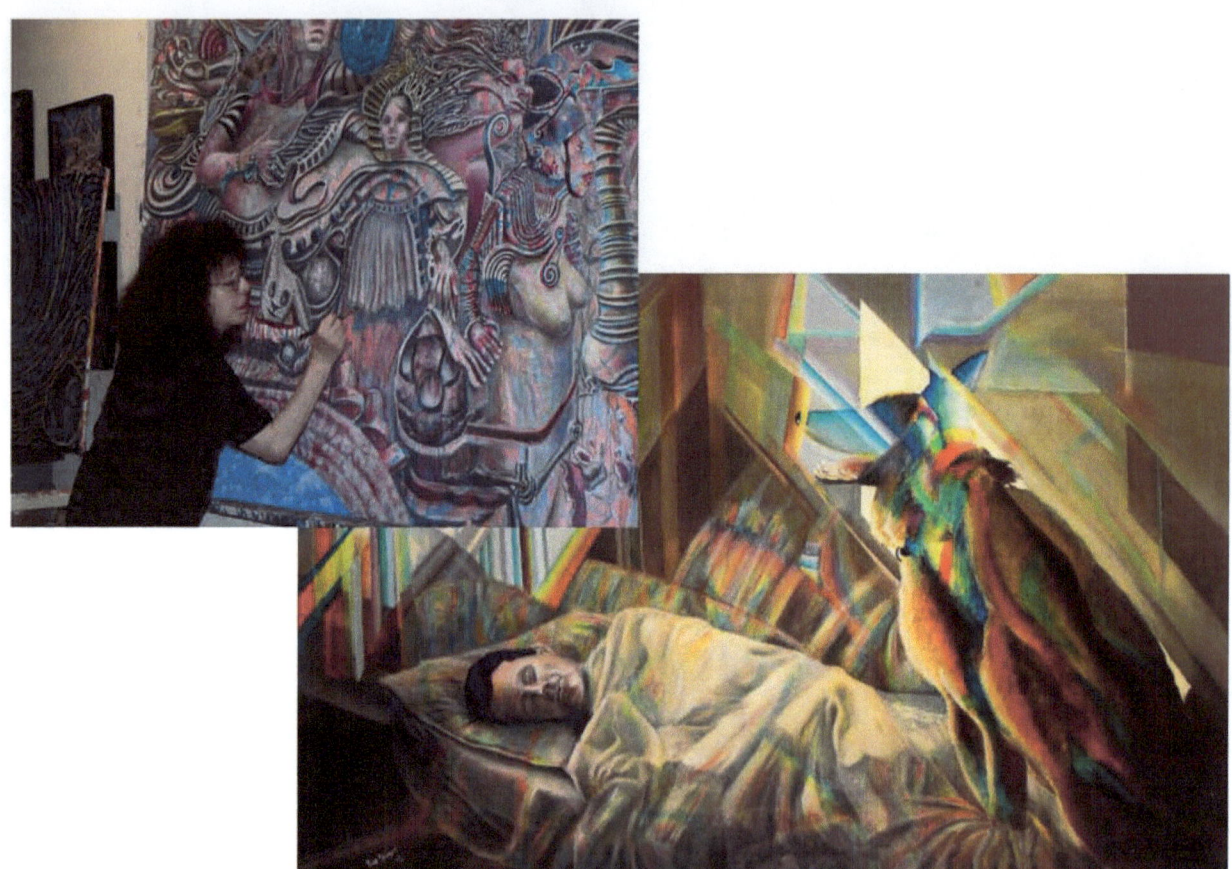

Olga Spiegel likes to improvise with free flowing images & color that creates associations to uncover a mysterious universe. Olga was brought up and trained in Europe, and now lives has her studio in New York. Her work has evolved from the abstract and optical energy fields influences of the 1960s through later study of the Old Master's technique with Ernst Fuchs, to her current unique visionary alphabet, that has lately included computer, digital paintings. Nurtured by Psychedelic Art, European Fantastic Realism, Surrealism and Science Fiction, her art points to an inner process, a chemical visual interaction were the inner self's, messages are deciphered through images and symbols taking the viewer into an edgy realm of realism and unnamable forms. Ancient icons, space-age imagery with metaphysical overtones, that reveal an evolutionary flowering, nature and its organisms populated into myriad of forms. Her work has shown in many galleries and private collections in Europe and America.

"Anything imagined can be made real – given sufficient genius" Brian Hubert & Kevin J. Anderson

Miguel Tio

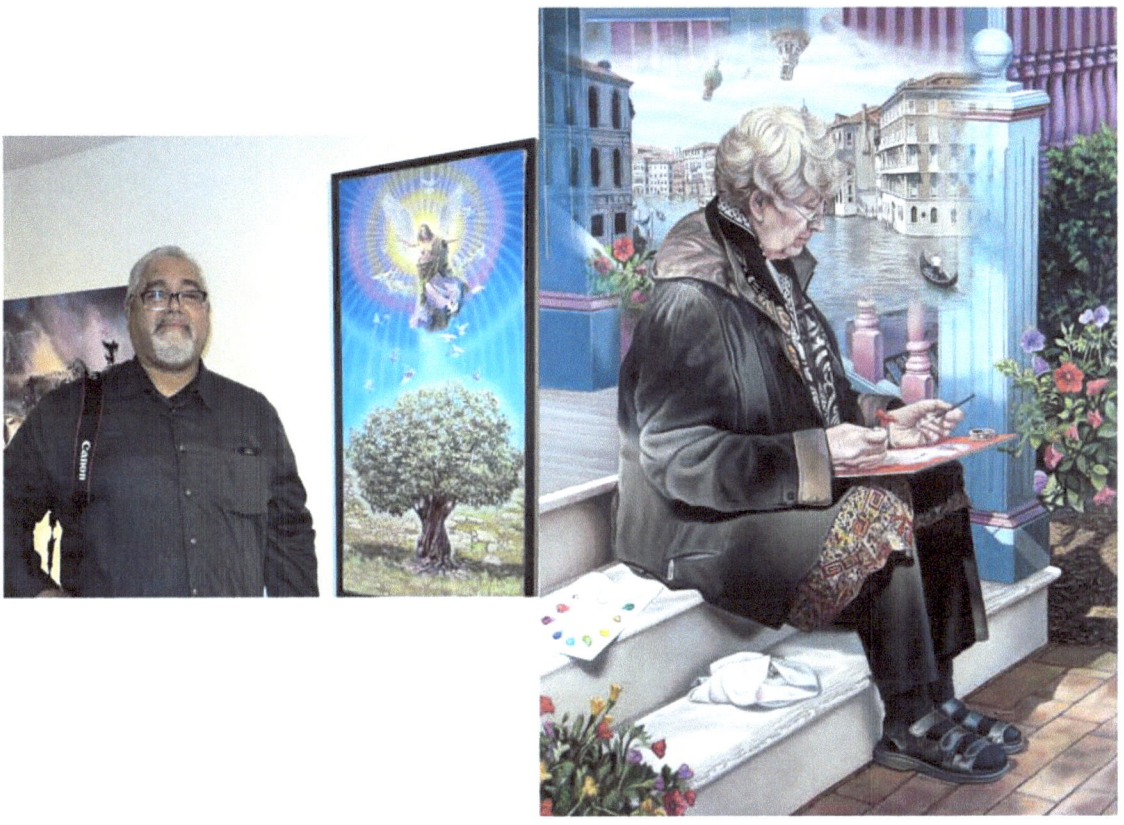

Miguel Tió, creates work that entices the eye and reward the mind. Miguel being a native of the Dominican Republic, began his studies of painting with the Dominican artist Elias Delgado as well as the Escuela Nacional de Bellas Artes. A move to New York in 1994 led him to Izquierdo Studio Ltd. for film and Television Production, window displays, opera and theater, which had a great influence on his artwork. In 2006 he studied the Mische technique with the very well known artist Brigid Marlin. His paintings show a dramatic and complex portraiture, irresistibly sensual and visionary, which exploits scale and luminosity without eschewing the personal and the poetical. He has done eight solo shows, the latest, "Now and After" at the Center for Latino Arts at Rutgers University. Has participated in group shows in Austria, France, England, Germany, Italy, Denmark, Sweden, Japan, North Cyprus, Australia, India, Mexico, Canada and the United States.

"The highest level of imagination is not to devise what has no existance, but rather to perceive what really exists, though unseen by the outward eye.. not creation, but insight."   Henry Wadsworth

Michael Coleman

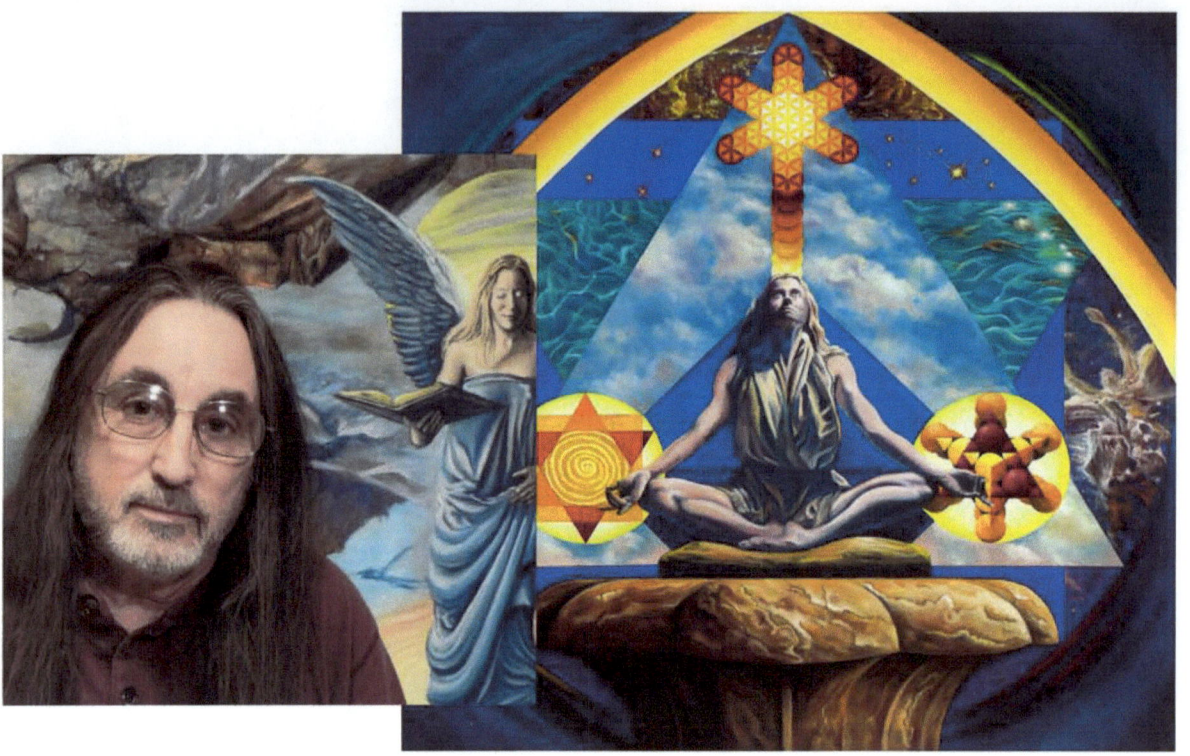

Born in Kansas City, Missouri, Michael Coleman has studied and created art his entire life. He Bachelor of Fine Arts is from at Louisiana Tech University. Michael moved to New Mexico in the mid 90s to expand his artistic options He worked on many projects creating murals, 3 dimensional art, graphics, for clients nationwide such as Paris Casino, Hollywood Casinos and an interesting 2 year project for the Imus Ranch for Kids with Cancer in New Mexico. Michael Coleman began his art education career in the late 90's by teaching for a private commercial art college. In 2002 he taught Fine Art at Bernalillo High School near Albuquerque. In 2005 he received a Master of Art in Education degree from the College of Santa Fe. He has also taught high and middle school Art in Dulce, New Mexico, on the Jicarilla Apache Reservation, and art education as an Associate Instructor at the University of Phoenix's Albuquerque campus. He has now come full circle.

"Imagination is the unique capacity to in some way connect with the invisible patterns of energy (spirit) hidden behind the conscious constructs of our perceptions, and bring forth an individual artistic expression of that experience."

William Otto

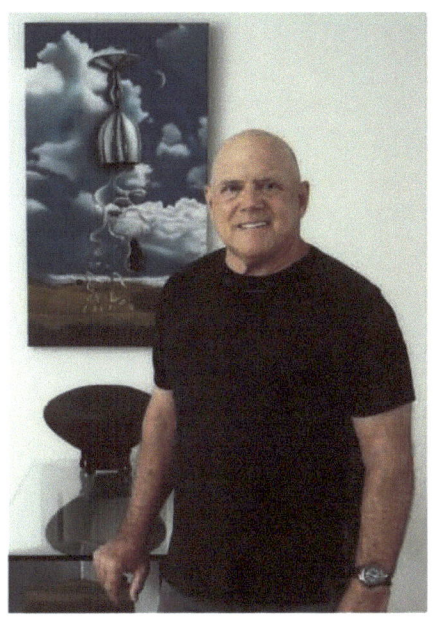
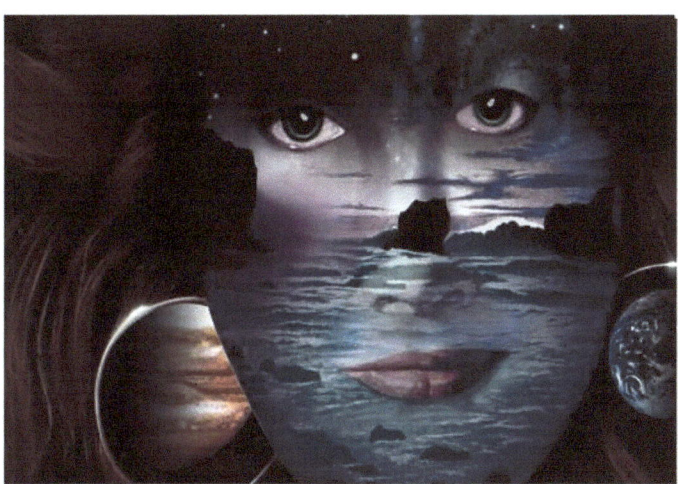

William feels his work is a vision of the world seen through the prism of the dream experience, reflecting invisible sources of energy and spirit. His first explorations into these experiences began as a Franciscan monk in the mid-1960s through the early 1970s. Although pursuing a career as a religious cleric did not result in a lifelong vocation, it initiated the exploration of religious traditions, mythologies, and cultures. This became the foundation for a master's degree in studio art from California State University, and a thesis titled 'An Alchemical Vision of Imagery', with bibliographic references citing comparative mythologies and the archetypal psychology of Carl Jung. "My journey begins with the infinity of nature, of which we are an integral part. The natural world that presents itself in the familiar forms of images, objects, places, and whole complexity of life, is itself my laboratory for developing a surreal, visionary expression to portray the whole of nature as a consciousness of infinite dimensions, forever mysterious and ineffable."

"The imagination is a palette of bright colors. You can use it to touch up memories — or you can use it to paint dreams. ~ Robert Brault

Irene Vincent

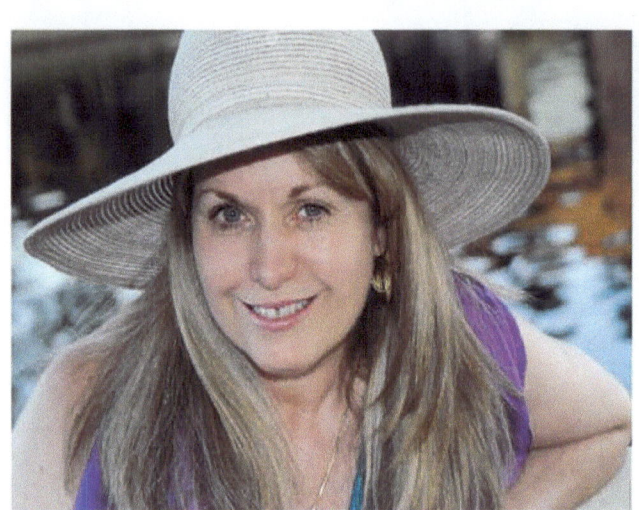
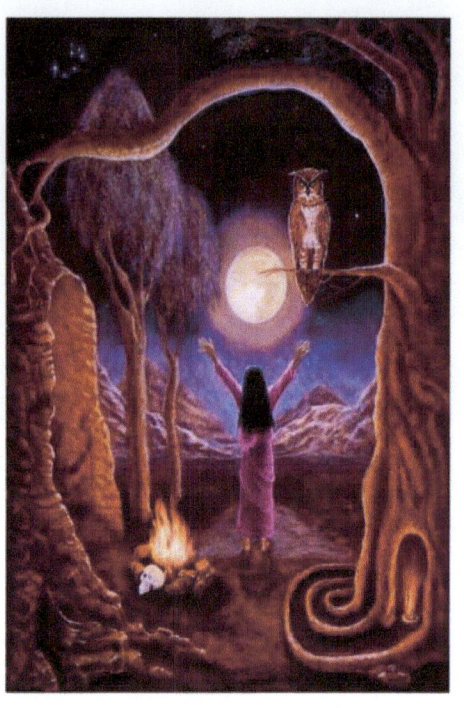

For over 45 years, Irene Vincent has painted visionary and mystical art, inspired from dreams, visions, sacred contemplations and spontaneous experimentation.
Studying symbols and dream interpretations led her to study her art in a similar way that brought a consciousness to the process, a way for her soul to awakenArt, imagination, and dreams intertwined with her waking life, giving it a new clarity. This clarity guided her to contemplate, what would an image of "love" look like. This thought created new paintings and drew enlightened yogi's, shamans, and other loving spiritual beings into her life, causing her to value her soul's evolution and the evolution of all souls. Dreams beaconed her tto travel to sacred sites around the world to pyramids, temples, ancient ruins, and to art museums.
She has traveled to Europe, Greece, Egypt, United States, Canada, Mexico, South America, Peru, Bolivia, Guatemala, Columbia, Jamaica, Tahiti, Thailand, Bali and India. From her travels she has gain an appreciation for the beauty in the diversity of cultures and the sacredness of mother earth's energy centers.Today, Irene teaches painting, paints, and is writing a spiritual trilogy memoir. 'Revealing – 'The Evolution of an Artist's Soul ' is Irene's first book of a trilogy. Her second book is 'Alchemy of Love'.

"The imagination is the goal of history I see culture as an effort to literally realize our collective dream."
Terrance McKenna

Liba Stambollion

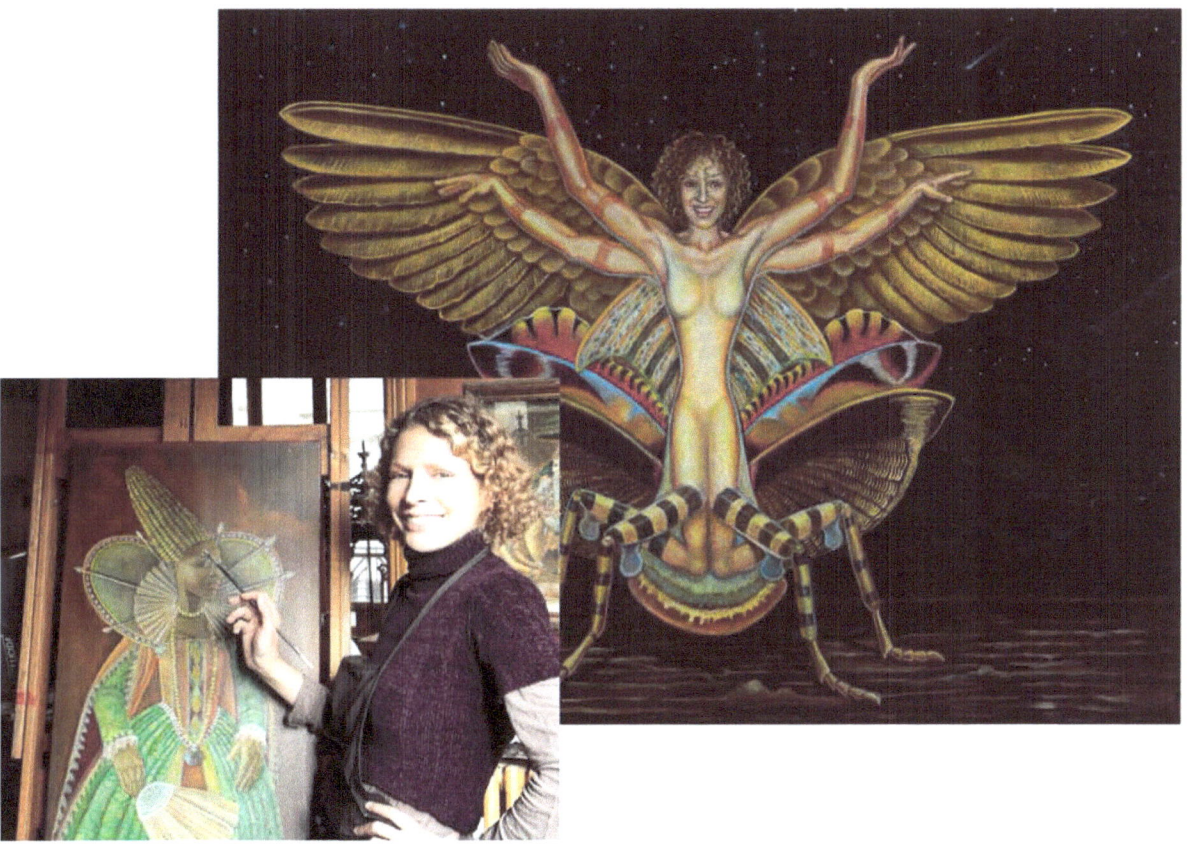

Liba WS's sacred art is sourced through her dreams, meditations, vision quests and her relationship with nature. She was born to American parents but grew up in South East Asia. She moved to the USA in her teenage years where she did a year of art and environmental studies at Simons Rock of Bard College and later received a scholarship from the School of the Art Institute of Chicago. She graduated in 1988 and stayed in Chicago exhibiting, teaching art and working for a cabinet maker. She has been living in Paris since 1993 where she paints, writes, makes books and designs furniture. Liba has been making handmade books & small collaborative artist editions for over twenty years. She launched Dreams and Divinities which unites visionary artists and showcases an eclectic mix of creativity through a series of books and exhibitions around the world. She is inspired and resonates with the message of Love from people of all cultures and from all ages.

"There is not rules of architecture for a castle in the clouds."   G.K. Chesterton

Lyne Lafontaine

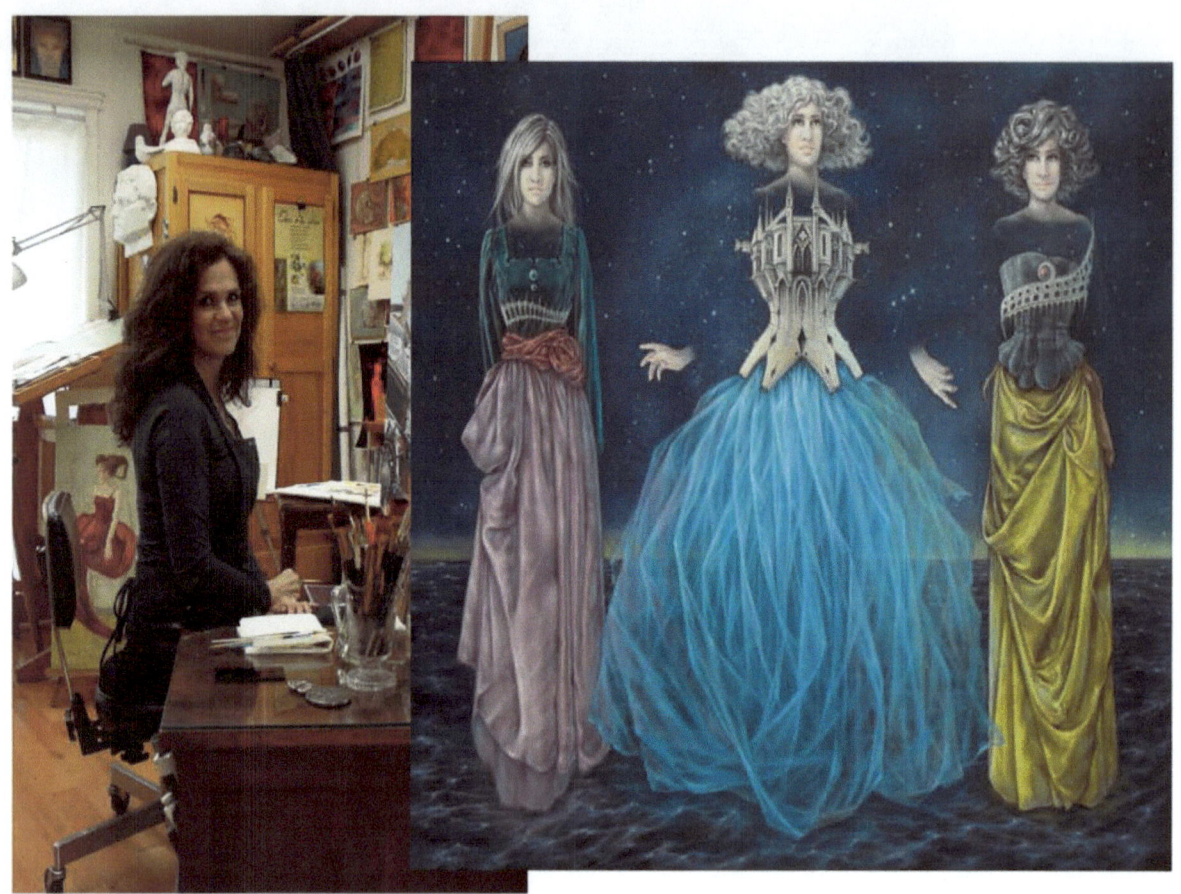

Lyne says of her work "Between reality and imaginary, I explore a world where human faces are at the center of my artworks." Lyne's universe moves around symbolism, fantasy, and femininity. Sensitivity and liberty must prevail upon all. For her facial expressions and human feelings have always been a great fascination and an endless source of inspiration. Lyne has been self- taught drawing since a very early age. It is with wonder and astonishment that she realizes to what extent fluidity can come from the simple line of a pencil. She experiments with oil painting techniques which proves to be fascinating for the details, wealth of material and color depth. Drawing and oil painting are her preferred mediums. They give her the array of possibilities that she is looking for. She feels this avenue is vital for her.

"It is frightfully difficult to know anything about fairies, and almost the only thing for certain is where there are fairies there are children" J. M. Barrie
Peter Pan in Kensington Garden

Joanne St. Cyr

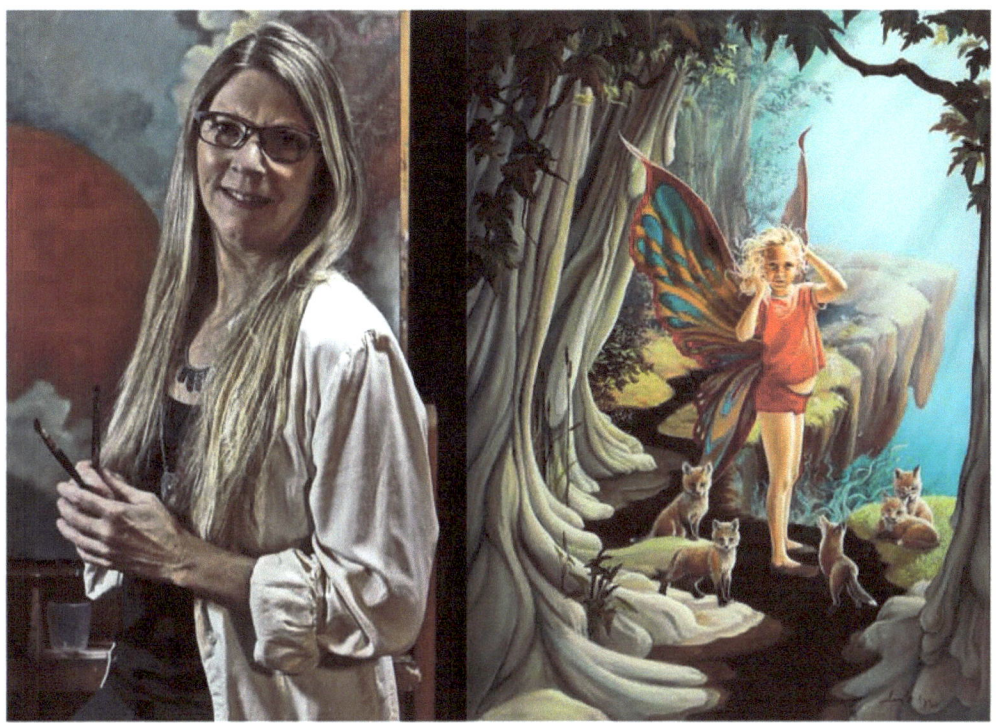

Born in Montreal, it is at a very young age that she discovered her love for drawing. It is with originality and a full imagination that she is initiated to painting in oils. From then on she will try to paint in the way of our great Renaissance Masters. But it is in the deepest roots of her imagination that she will discover her own style, that she will re-invent new and symbolic worlds from her philosophy and life experiences. She worked as a Graphic Artist before settling down in Quebec City in 1990 where she has been teaching painting and drawing. She has studied Fine Art at Concordia University and UQAM in Montreal, Canada. After many years of exploring different mediums she now switches from oil to acrylic whenever the mood dictates the inspiration of the moment.

"You are a divine being, you matter, you count. You come from realms of unimaginable power and light and you return to them." Terance McKenna

Rosemary Stehlik

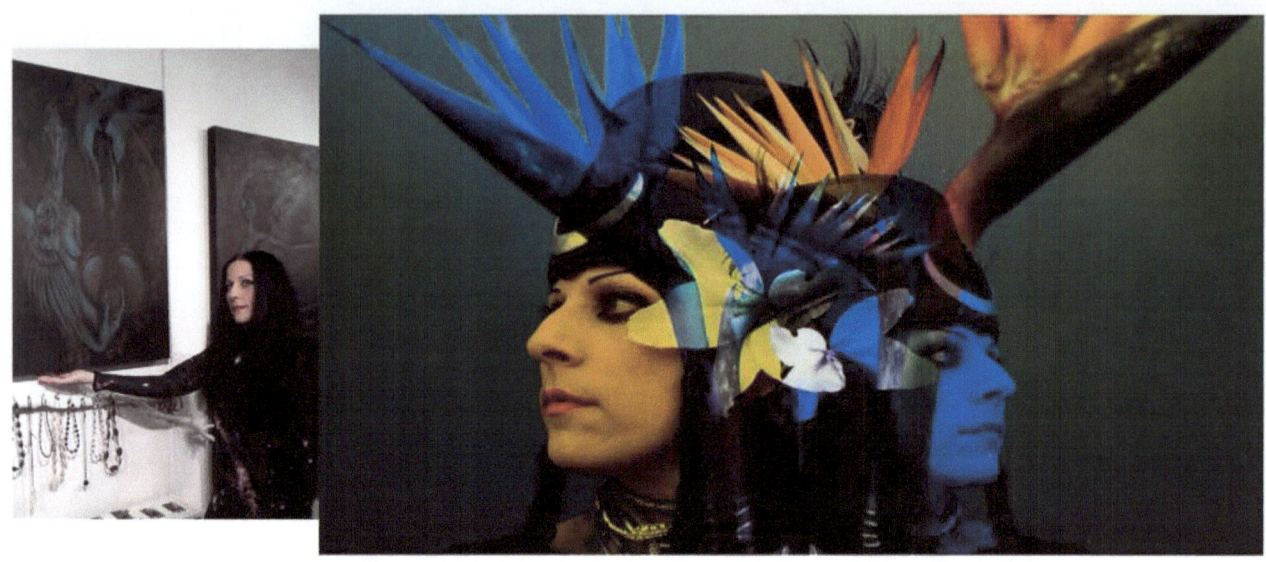

Rosemary Stehlik Photography by Kate Young (Kate Young is a Calgary born, Toronto based artist. Her practice is expressed through photography, film and art direction.)

Rosmarinus Stehlik is a Living Work of Art in Perpetual Motion. She is a Multidisciplinary Artist and graduate of McMaster University in Canada with two Honours B.A Degrees in Fine Arts and Art History, respectively; and a minor degree in Religious Studies. Her Life is defined by the engagement of the Mysteries, such as Honoured placements in O.T.O, and the Full Path engagement of Practice in Shaolin Kung FU, culminating with her medal-award winning participation in the 10th Zhengzhou International Wushu Championship in China in October of 2014. She is the student of 35th Generation Shaolin disciple Shi Chang Dao, and was selected to become an instructor of the Shaolin Temple Quanfa Institute. Rosmarinus Stehlik was born a Visual Artist. She has participated Group Art Exhibits all over the World, Including California, Cusco Peru, Toronto and now, BALI.

"If you have a dream, don't just sit there. Gather courage to believe that you can succeed and leave no stone unturned to make it a reality." Ropleen

Chris Dyer

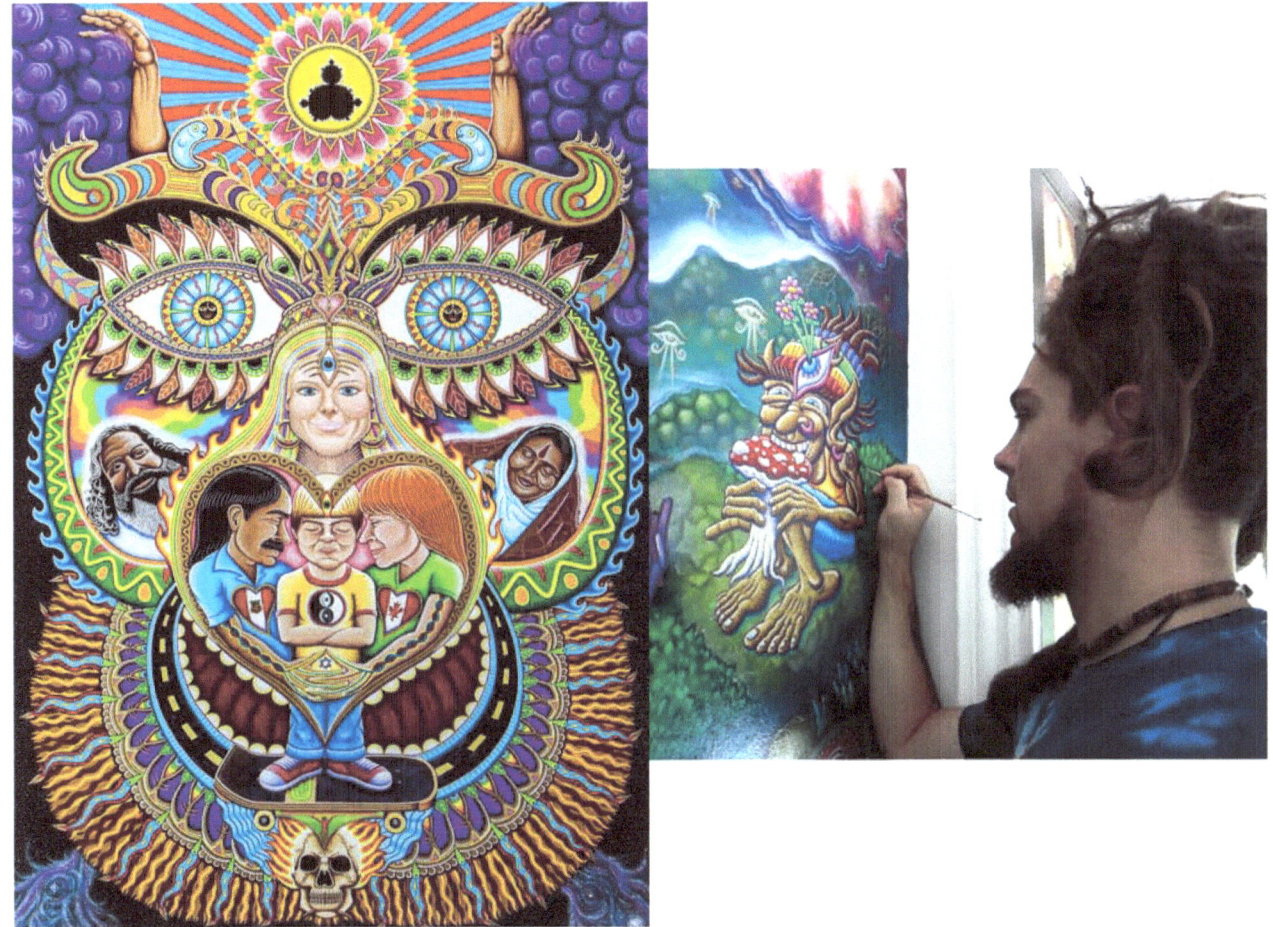

Chris Dyer is a Peruvian artist, who lived in Lima Peru till the age of 17 and is now living in Montreal. His main objective is to do his part in raising humanity's consciousness. He believes delivering positive images to the youth, via the skateboard graphics he produces, is the powerful seed that can manifest a happier reality for us all. His art now transcends just skateboards as there are so many things in our world that could use some extra color. He hopes to pass on a positive message to the youth with these expressions. Chris has traveled all over the world in search for his own answers to life. As for his Fine Arts Career, he has had solid solo and group exhibitions in lands like Peru, Mexico, Belgium, San Francisco, Seattle, British Columbia, Toronto, Quebec City and of course Montreal. All this travel experiences adds to the cultural richness of his work.

"The world of reality has its limits: the world of imagination has no boundaries." Jean Jacques Rousseau

Margot Bussiere

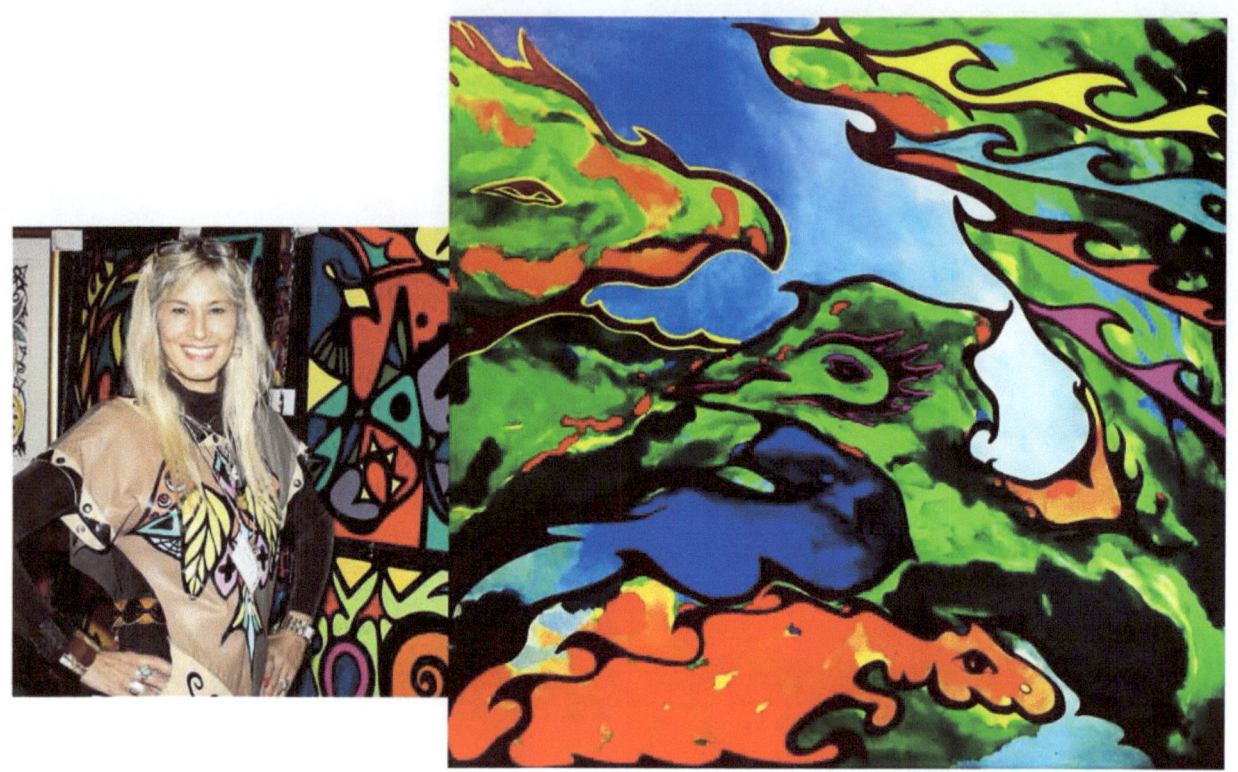

Margot is an artist that likes spontaneity and creativity. She has developed some techniques on plywood that have freestyle art on them. She responds to the environment around her with sentiments and emotion. Her artistic career is characterized by spontaneous and authentic expression of her reality as woman, mother and artist. She says "I explore my femininity with in all aspects of my art." Margot has developed several techniques using 3-D, Grafftag, Oil on Plywood and Freestyle. The 3-D is carried out on female plastic molds fixed on canvas, Her artistic sensibility is directly connected to her environment and she answers these impulses creation in her paintings expressing the feelings and emotsions that she sees throughout her life journey.

"Engaging our individual expression, using imagination to inform, expand, and guide us, we can begin to return to Eden."
(Suzanne Beth Stinnett) Little Shifts

Jerome Bertrand

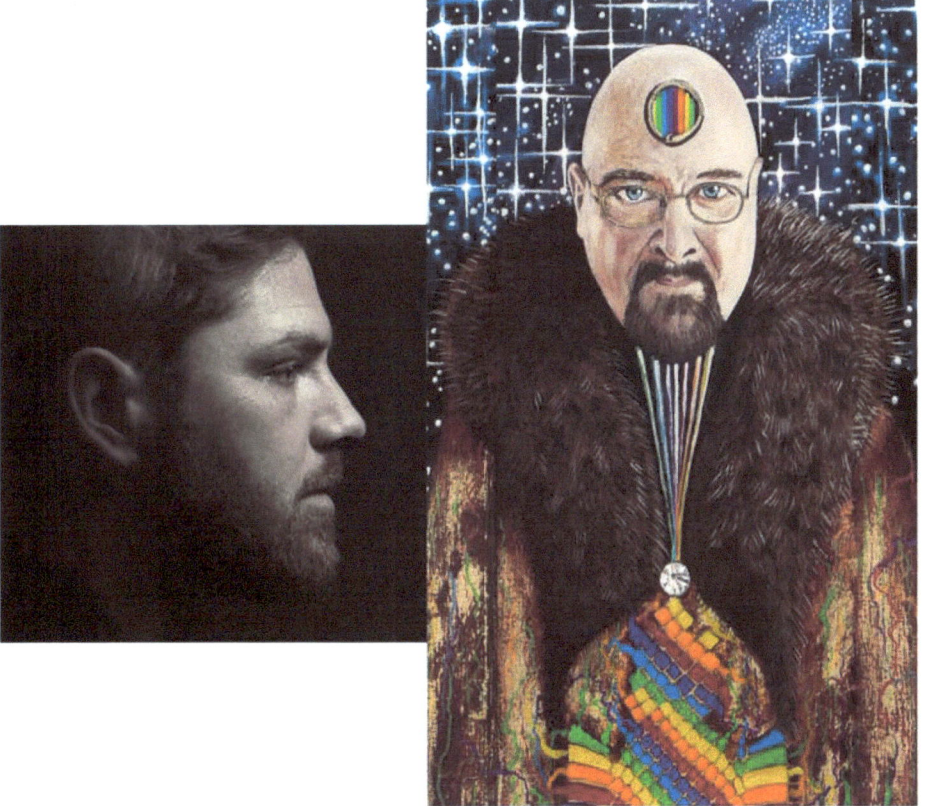

Inspired by the mythologies of different cultures
Jerome mostly paints portraits of his friends in symbolic contexts. In fact, his visionary art takes on ancient tales with a revitalizing way of looking at his entourage from the inside. His focus on small formats and passion for detail is what gave him the opportunity to be an art teacher regardless of his young age. With a strong technique in drawing combined with a clever use of colors, he can accurately project his visions. Currently working from his studio in Montreal, he is eager to show the world what's boiling in his mind.

"If the winds of fortune are temporarily blowing against you, remember that you can harness them and make them carry you toward your definite purpose, through the use of your imagination." Napoleon Hill

Georgina Smith

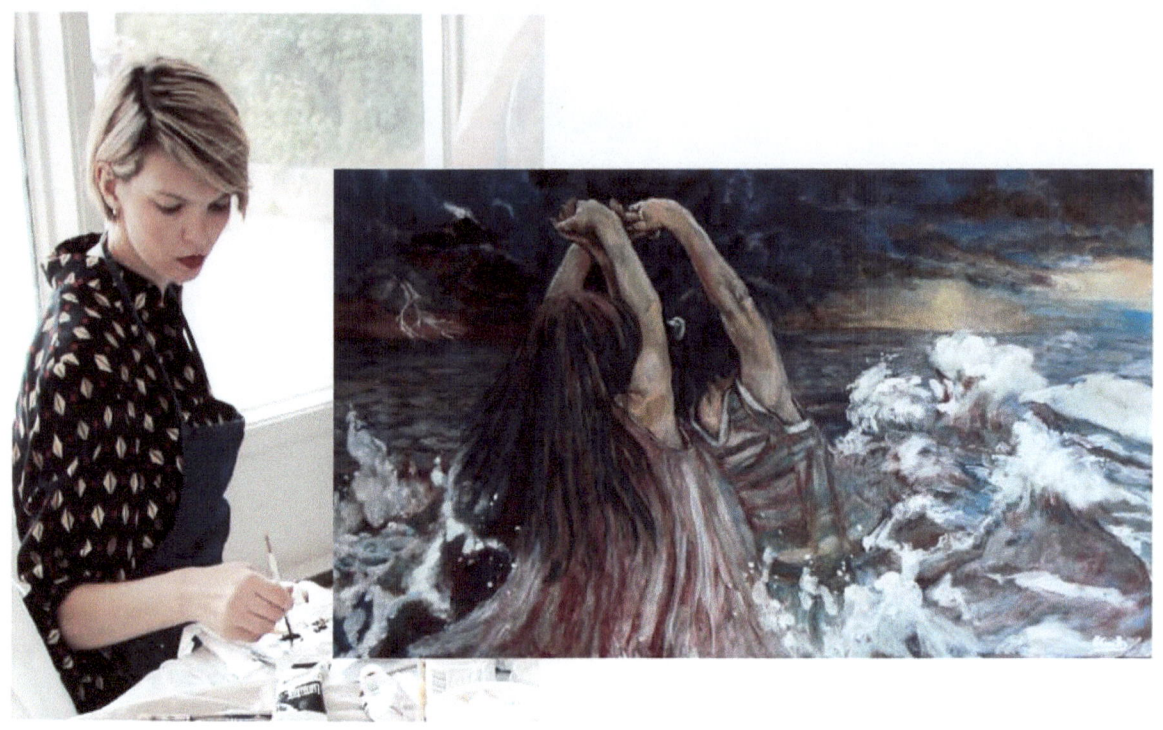

Georgina's artworks are the looking glass of her subconscious. Her work is intuitive, personal and very significant in her life. Symbols appear in her work, creating meaning and answering daily inquiry. She uses her art practice as therapy; as a way to make sense of life and its multiple situations. Her work is often said to be surrealist. She uses existing subjects and place them in surreal surroundings. Although, these subjects do not represent her physically, she considers her artworks as self portraits. They are symbols and portions of her life at the moment of their creation. She works closely with photography in her process. She works in transparent layers starting with a very loose sketch on the canvas or wood piece. During this process, she pays close attention to involuntary shapes that emerge and that may spark inspiration for other imagery or symbols. Each piece has its' own story and personal meaning.

"An imaginative mind is a place where you can find magic." Debasish Mridha

Dustyn Lucas

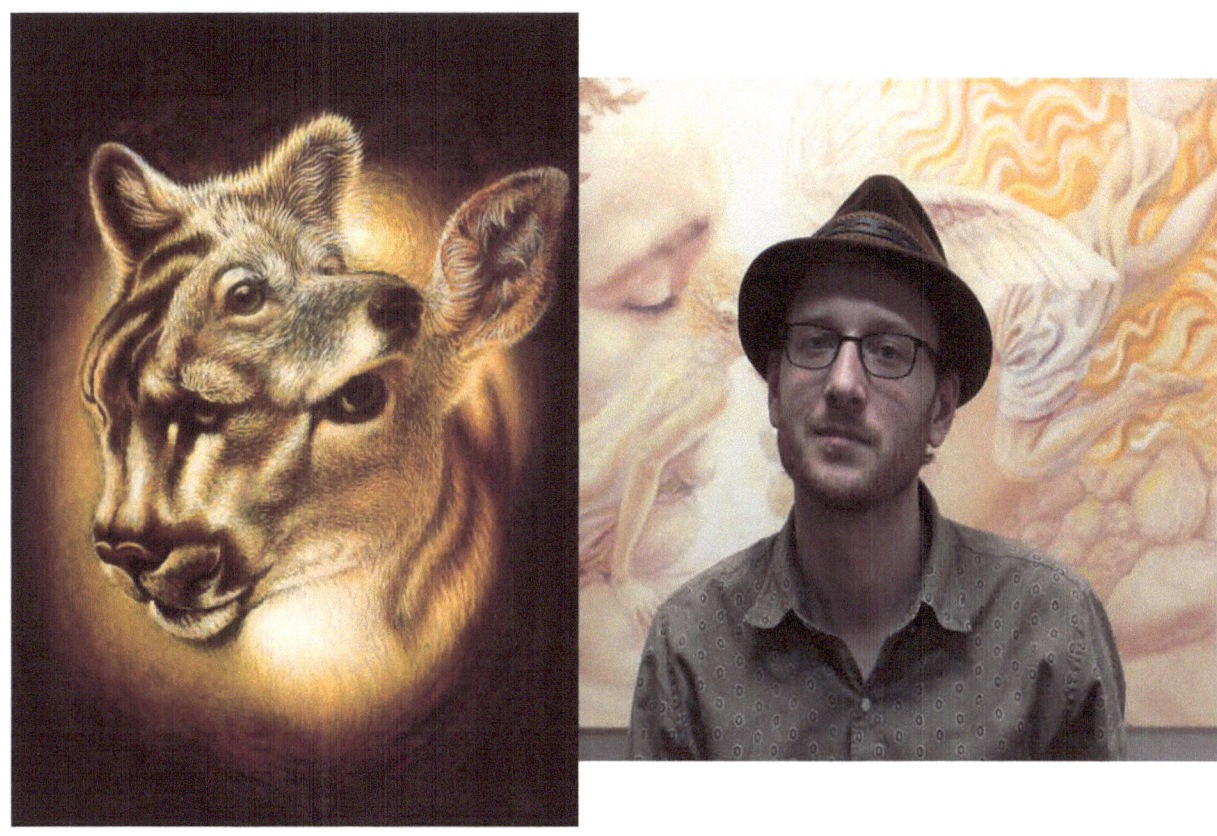

Dustyn Lucas is interested in Consciousness, Fractals, sacred geometry and lucid dreaming.
He is a 31-year-old native of Kingsville, Ontario — Canada's southernmost town — born in a family with a rich artistic heritage. He adopted painting shortly after his first steps and inherited his grandpa's tools of the trade after he passed away. While he studied at the Sheldon Arts Academy, his versatile skillsets which includes painting, sculpting, graphic design, and music were largely self- taught. Dustyn was the pianist of a folk / gypsy band entitled "The Unsettlers" that performed in various festivals such as Osheaga and the Montreal Jazz Fest in recent years but is currently in hiatus. Dustyn's boundless creativity, which at times stems from the dream world ensures a continuously shifting approach to the themes of fractals and visual puns. He is currently working on producing a series of visual koans (paradoxical riddle) inspired from Zen Buddhism.

"Never outgrow your imagination."
– Teresa Mummert

Ricky Schaede

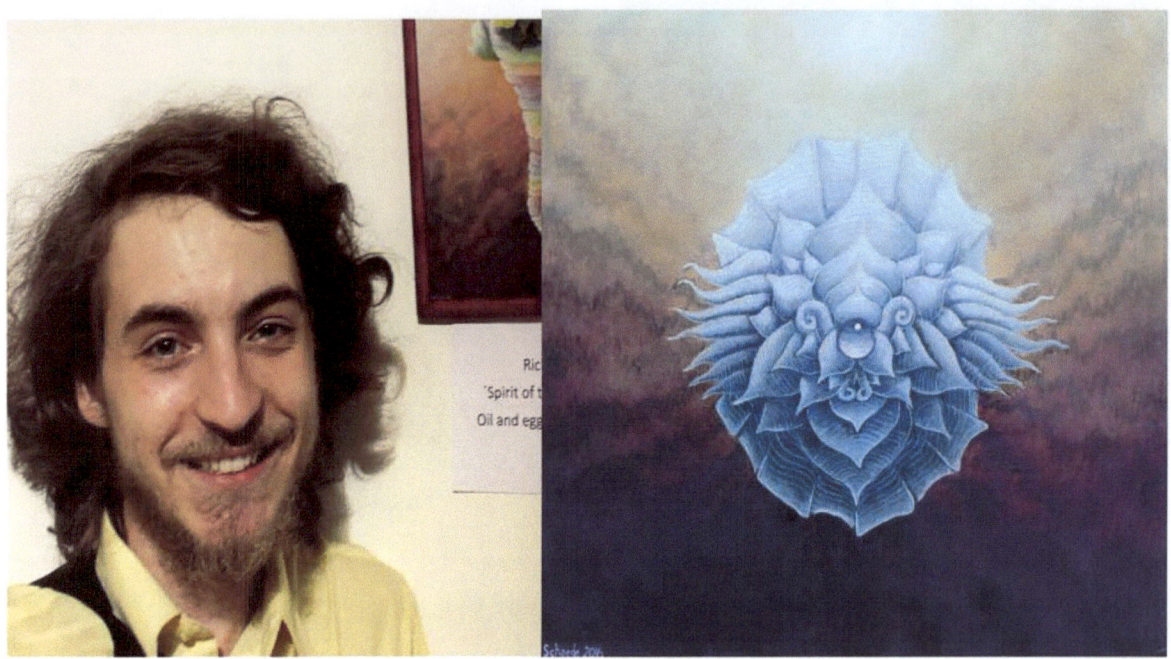

Ricky Schaede is a Canadian Artist passionately exploring the imagination and honouring the inner child.
It is his belief that the freedom of the inner child's expression is at the root of our happiness. His work stems from personal experiences and emotions, dreams, and imagination. He is inspired by world culture, icons, and imagery, and is constantly exploring such cultural input to nourish his visual language. His father introduced him to art at an early age, and a trip to Guatemala in 2012 unlocked his creativity as he participated in a series of sacred fire ceremonies. He has been making art since. In 2013 he co-founded Club Art Orangeville, a non profit dedicated to providing a safe space for local youth to experience the arts, and in the summer of 2015 & 2016 he travelled to Austria to study the mische technique. Working in acrylics, & oils, the mische technique, ink, graphite, and sculpture, his work explores mystical worlds, fantastic creatures, and divine situations as metaphors for the human experience. Schaede states that "the paintings I create are sparks of himself and the transformation he has experienced."

"Imagination does not become great until human beings, given the courage and the strength, use it to create.
(Maria Montessori)

Zeerka

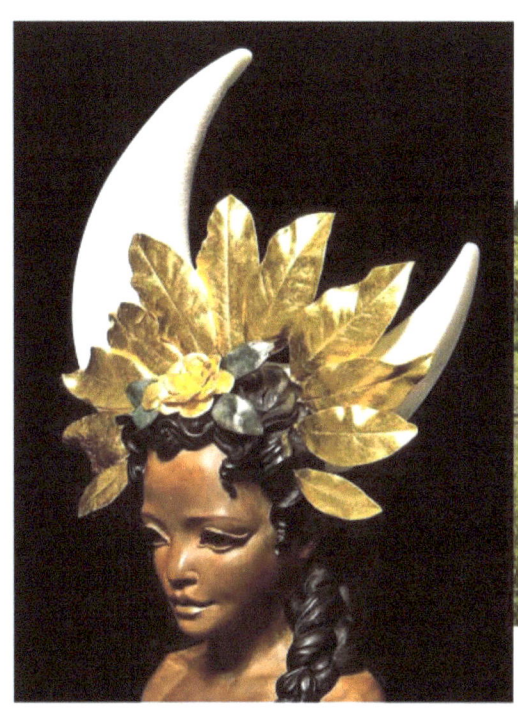
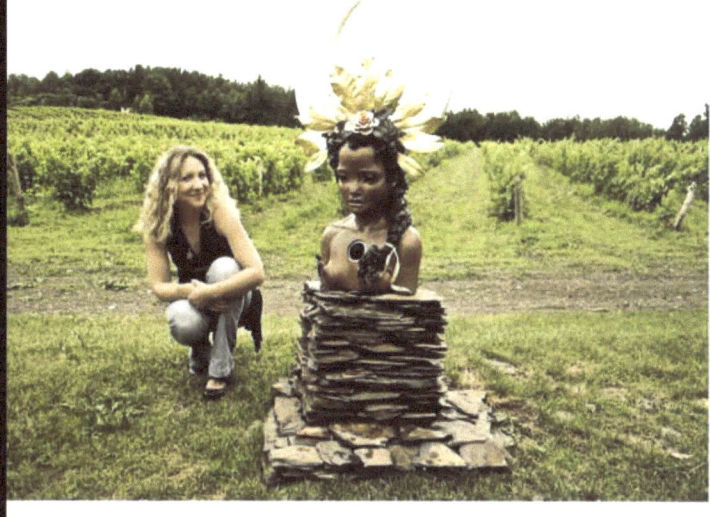

Zeerka was born in 1975 in Quebec, Canada.
Since childhood, she expressed his artistic gifts by the "Rudolf Steiner" method in the "Waldorf" of Montreal. The realization of her passion for sculpture occured in 1996, while doing her Visual Arts degree at the University of Sherbrooke. After commiting to doing sculpture in 2001, she travelled, studied and worked for many years between Quebec and Italy (Carrara & Pietrasanta). From 2003 to 2005, she was selected twice for scholarships from the Ministry of Foreign Affairs in Rome, where she worked on technical classic carving marble in Carrara & Pietrasanta, Italy. The artist has participated in cultural events and the international artistic communities. Zeerka says ...
"My heart beats to the rhythm of creative movement and cyclical from an intemporal and Universal illusive perception of time... always searching for "the way" to unify instead of " divide " our historical past with our present time. Today we tend to delete the beauty, the heart, magic and the sacred of life. I am at service to beauty; to others, to communities, Society and Humanity."

"Without freedom there is no creation."
Jiddhud Krishnamurti

Andrew Gonazlez

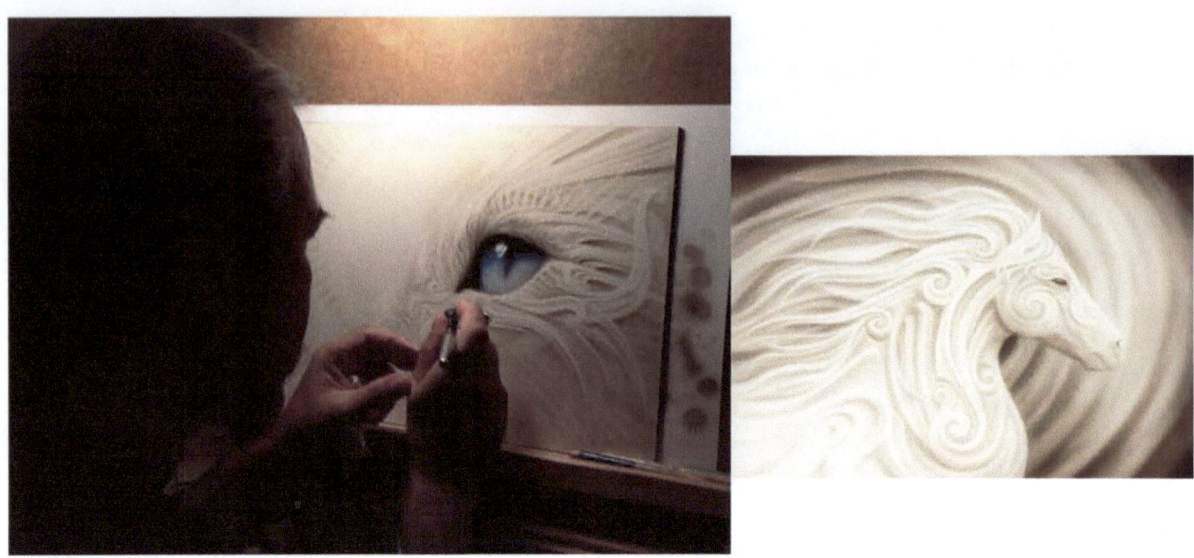

"My childhood preoccupation with dreams and imaginal worlds would soon lead me to the masters of imaginative painting. But it wasn't mere "fantasy" art that would call to me, but an art with a particular revelatory power. I longed for an art that would contemplate the jewel of wisdom hidden within and reveal the glory and mystery of being, an art sublimed with grace and beauty, subtle, yet profoundly ecstatic and mythically bold in its declaration. The augurs of this revelatory art that would initially inspire my imagination would be found within the visionary and mystical art traditions and disseminated within the movements of Symbolism, Art Nouveau, Surrealism and Fantastic Art. As a young teenager it was Dali's "Nuclear Mysticism" that first captivated my imagination, then followed by the preeminent work of Ernst Fuchs, William Blake and the mystical idealism of Jean Delville. And later as a young adult, the creative eye of my soul marveled at the prodigious possibilities brought forth by the ominous visions of H.R. Giger, the crystalline vistas of Robert Venosa and the transparent transfigurations of Alex Grey."

"Imagination is the only weapon in the war against reality"
C.S. Lewis   Alice in Wonderland

Fay Marineau

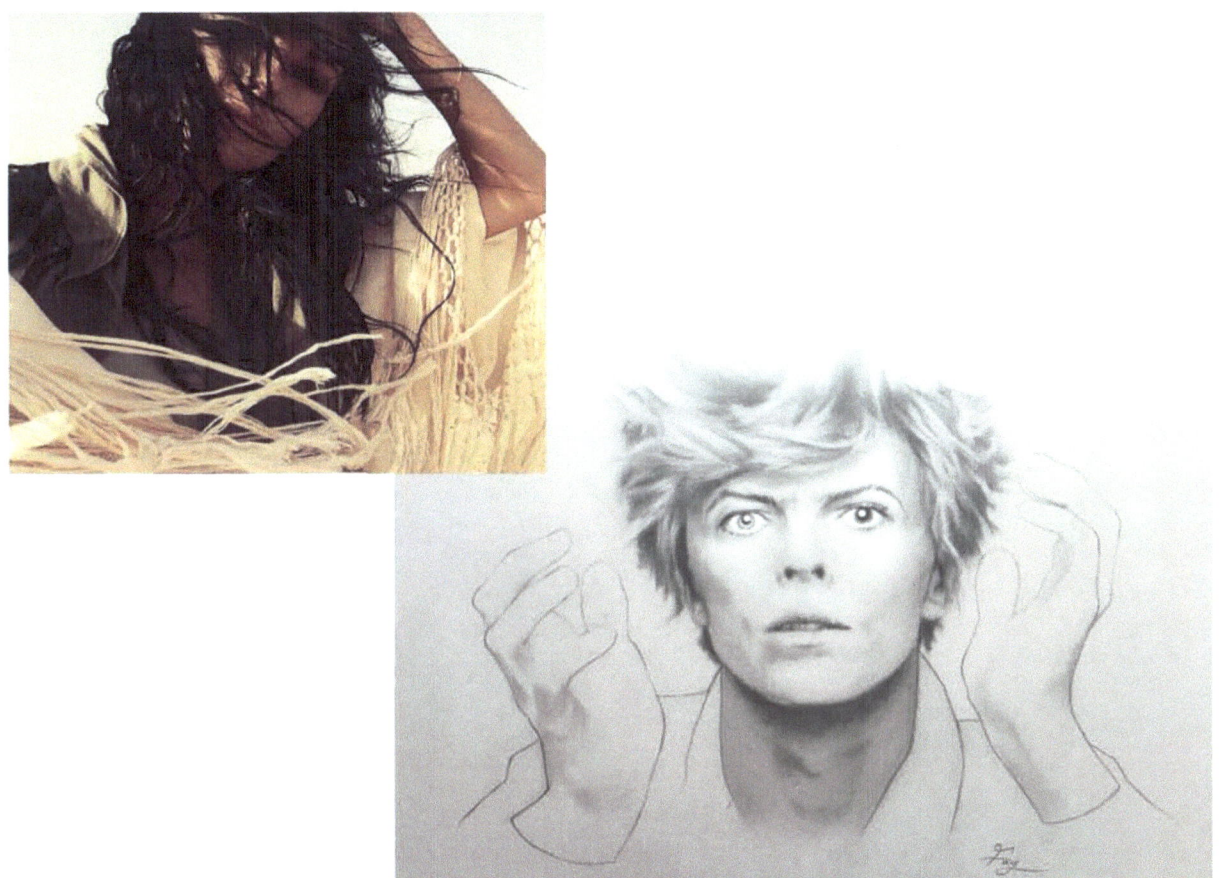

Fay has worked in art related fields for 10 years (graphic design, illustration, artistic makeup) Before she made the decision to get back to her first passion: Drawing and painting. She went and studied the old masters techniques for a year and started drawing again whenever she could find time, after this long hiatus.
She was invited to join the society for Art of Imagination in April 2016 and participated in her first art show in Cuzco, Peru in June. This experience was very inspiring and transforming for the artist. Her style can be described as figurative fantastical surrealism. She uses graphite and gold leaf mainly and gets her inspiration from mythology, music, culture and her numerous travels.

"Be free like a child. Let your imagination fly high. You must make it a point to surround yourself with the people who are like that."
(Dominco Mazza How to Find Your Passion)

Sylke Gande

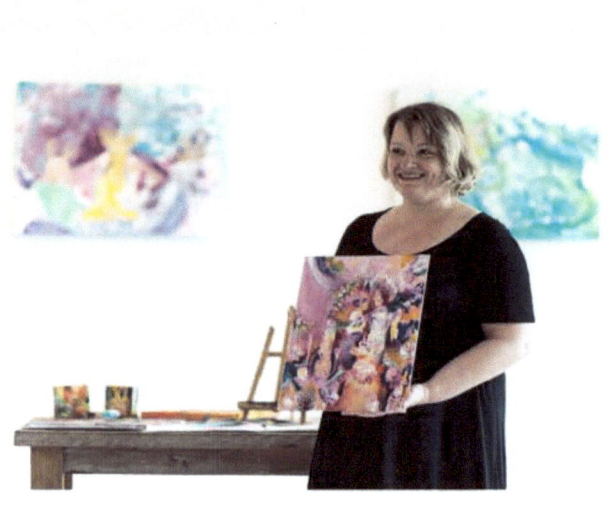
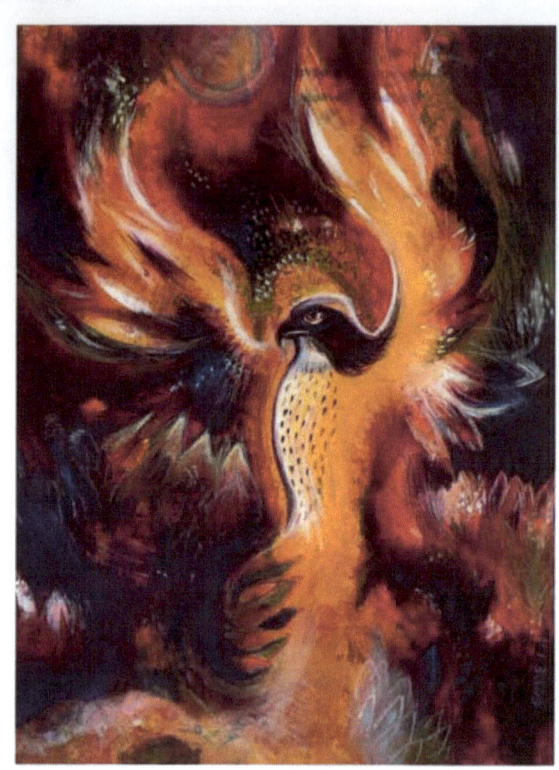

Sylke is an artist and graphic designer from Munich Germany. Using color is one of her strongest elements. She paints fast and spontaneous. The paper is the space to give life to the hidden unseen – important themes of the moment. The meaning comes later. Her paintings can be wild or calm, colorful or dark. You can find flying horses, a samurai, birds, mermaids, couples or a person alone. She has fun in turning the paper round during working, upside down – every way works.
Each side gives a new chance, new ideas and prospects.. Sylke has also been to the Spirit of Writing and Art in Bali three times, the first time she studied painting with Philip Rubinov Jacobsen, the next two times she contributed her talent in teaching Sacred Art with circular mandalas.

Art Show Bali - Imagination Reigns

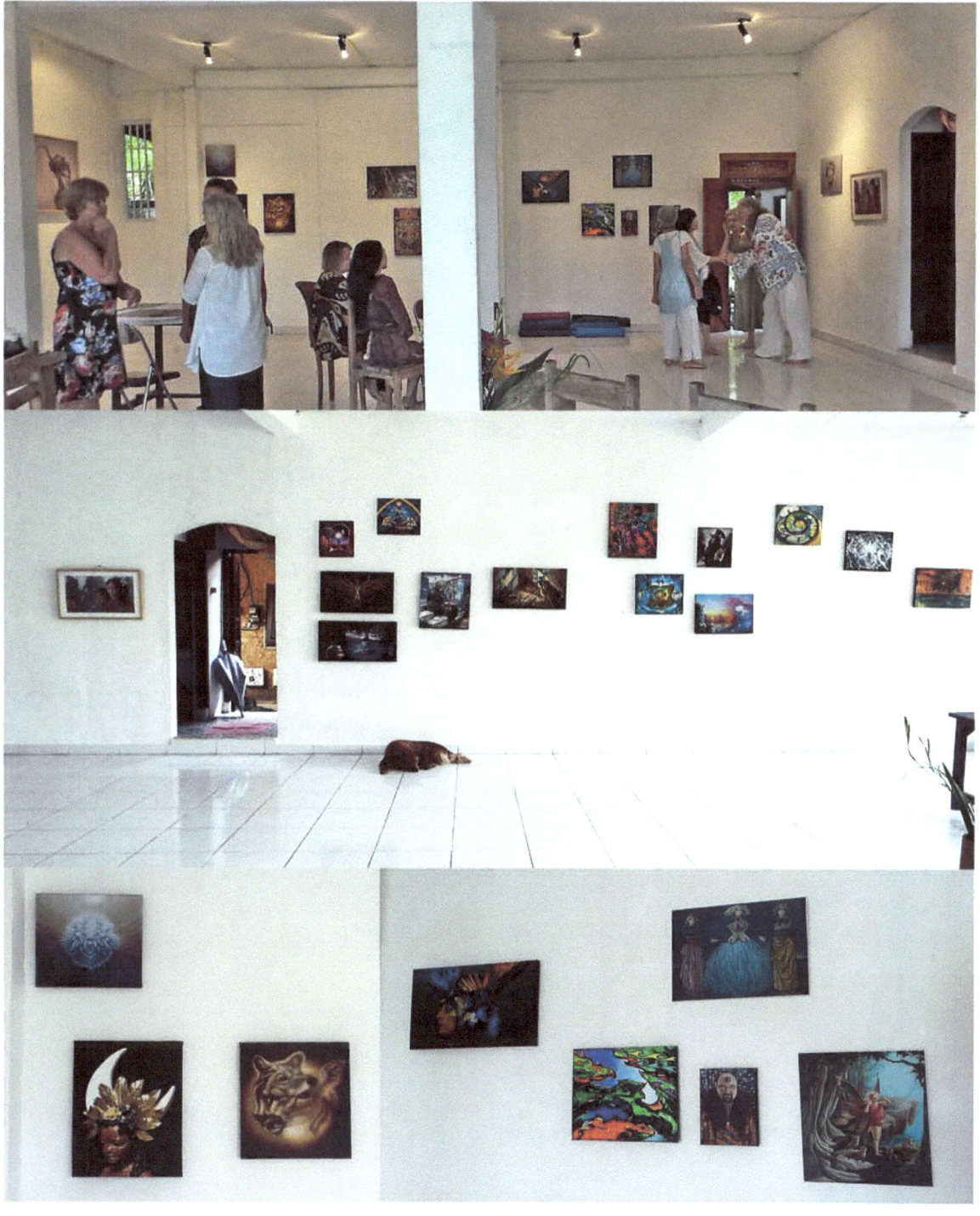

Group of artists at show
sylke Gande, Irene Vincent, Melissa Fay Marineau, Dale Bertand, Gusti Lanang, Made Sure, Aboetd Art

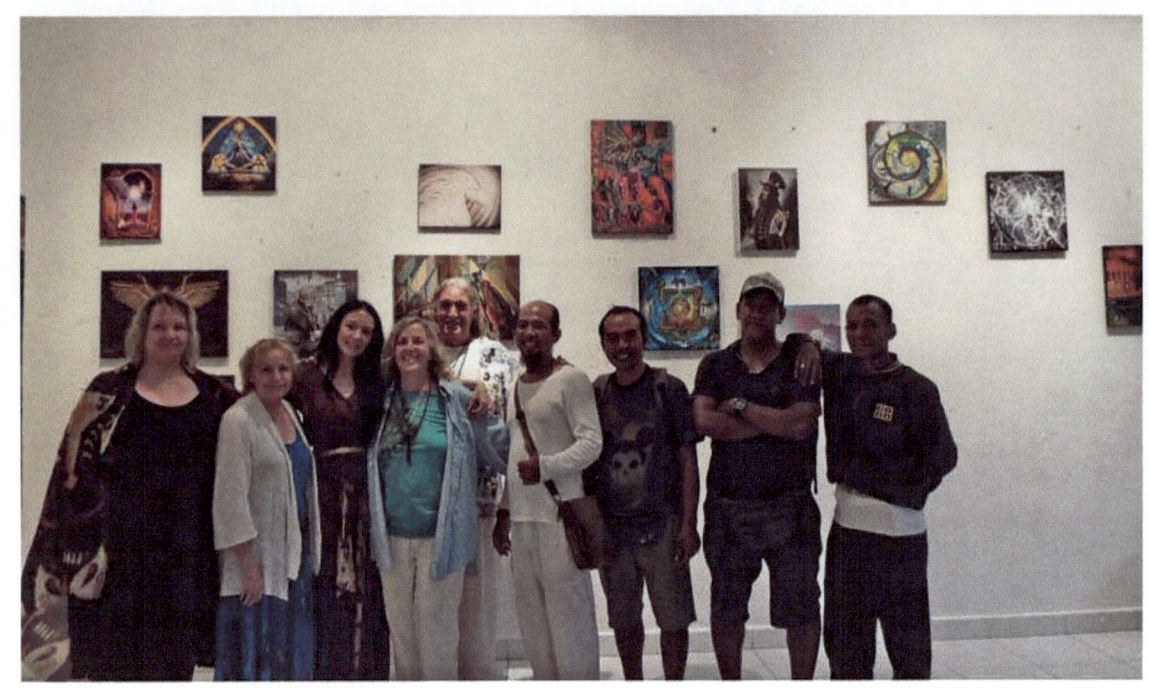

Della Burford's introduction
Della did an introduction to the show and told the history of the Society for Art of Imagination

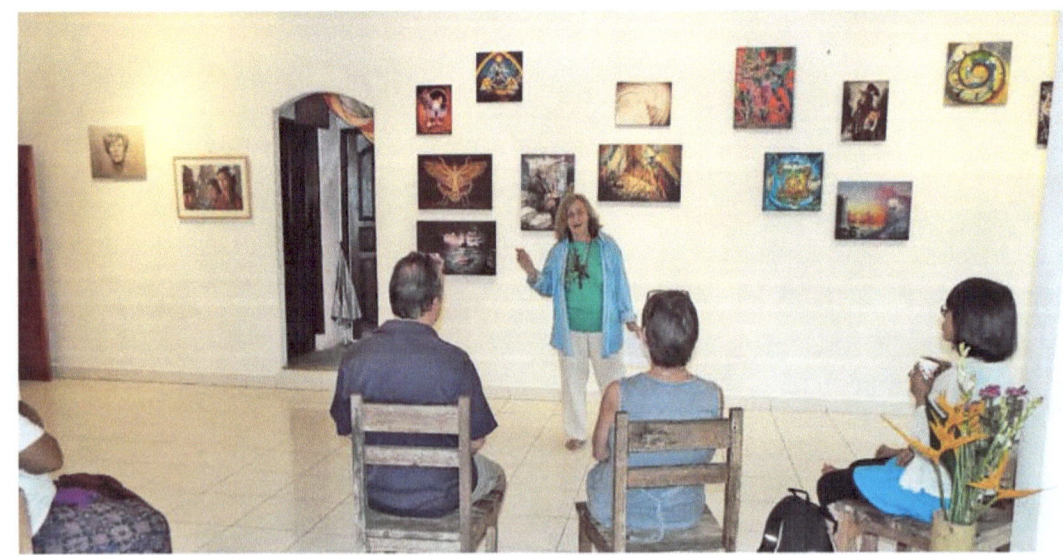

International artists at Opening:

Top photo: Margaritta from Norway, Karja from Bali, Della from Canada, Monica Kiraly from Hungary.
Bette Altshuler - Denmark, Gede Suryawan from Bali

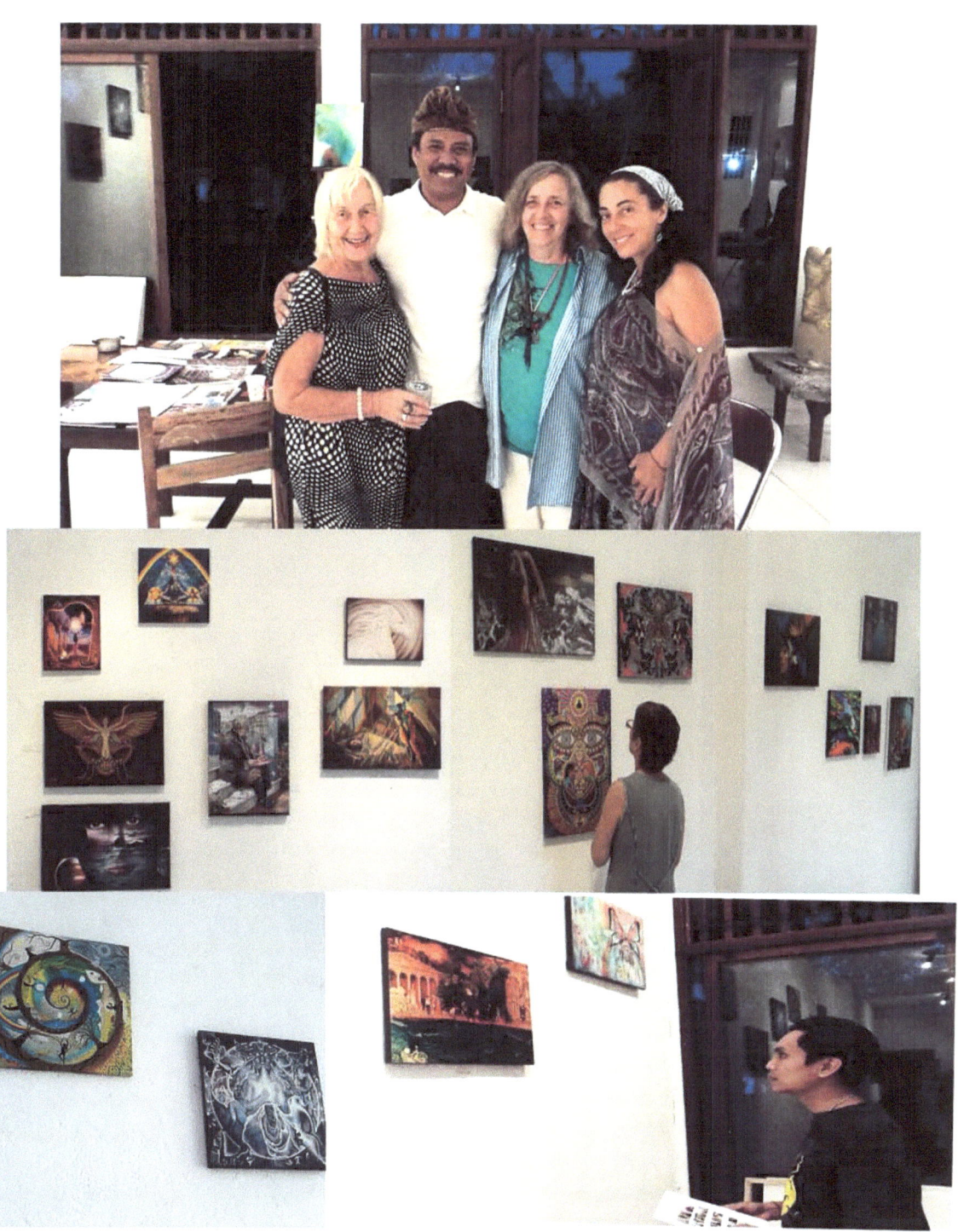

Della facilitated an acupressure -yoga class, & Inspiration class - Spirit Maps were created Top: Della Stella, Sylke, Karina, Irene & Melissa.
Below: Aboetd from Aboetd Art

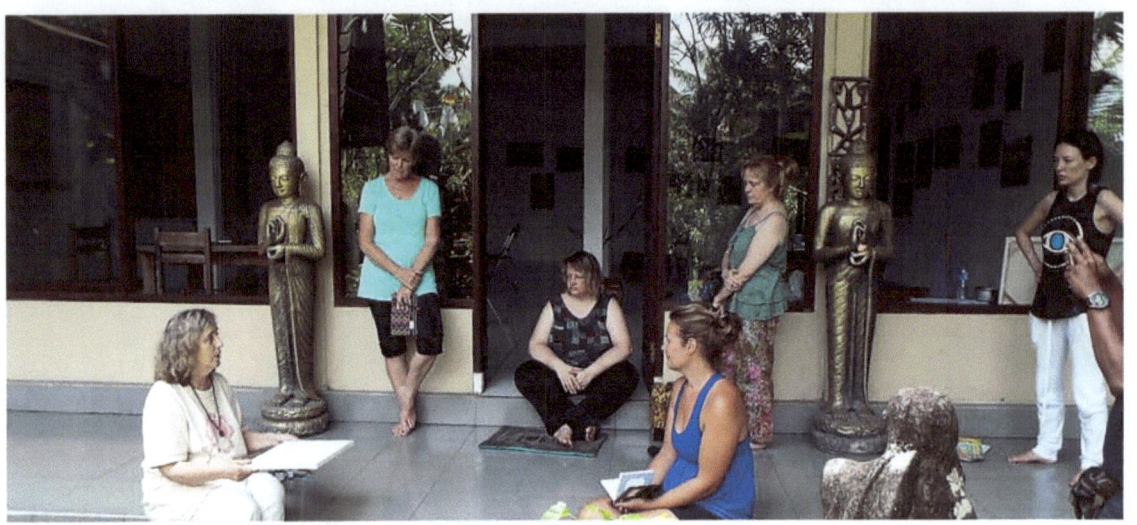

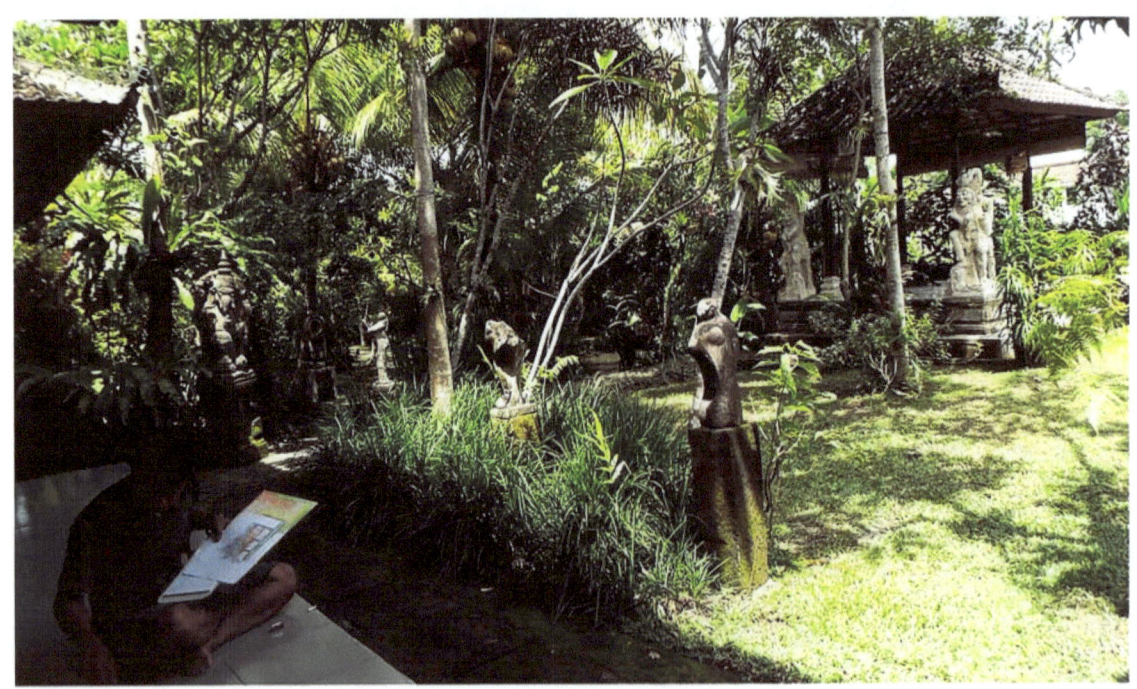

Dale Bertrand in Gallery of Art facilitating "Medicine Wheels".

Top: Dale, Melissa, Irene, Stella, Robbie, Karina Belwo: Dale, Norah, Robbie, Karian & Stella. Ryan visiting.

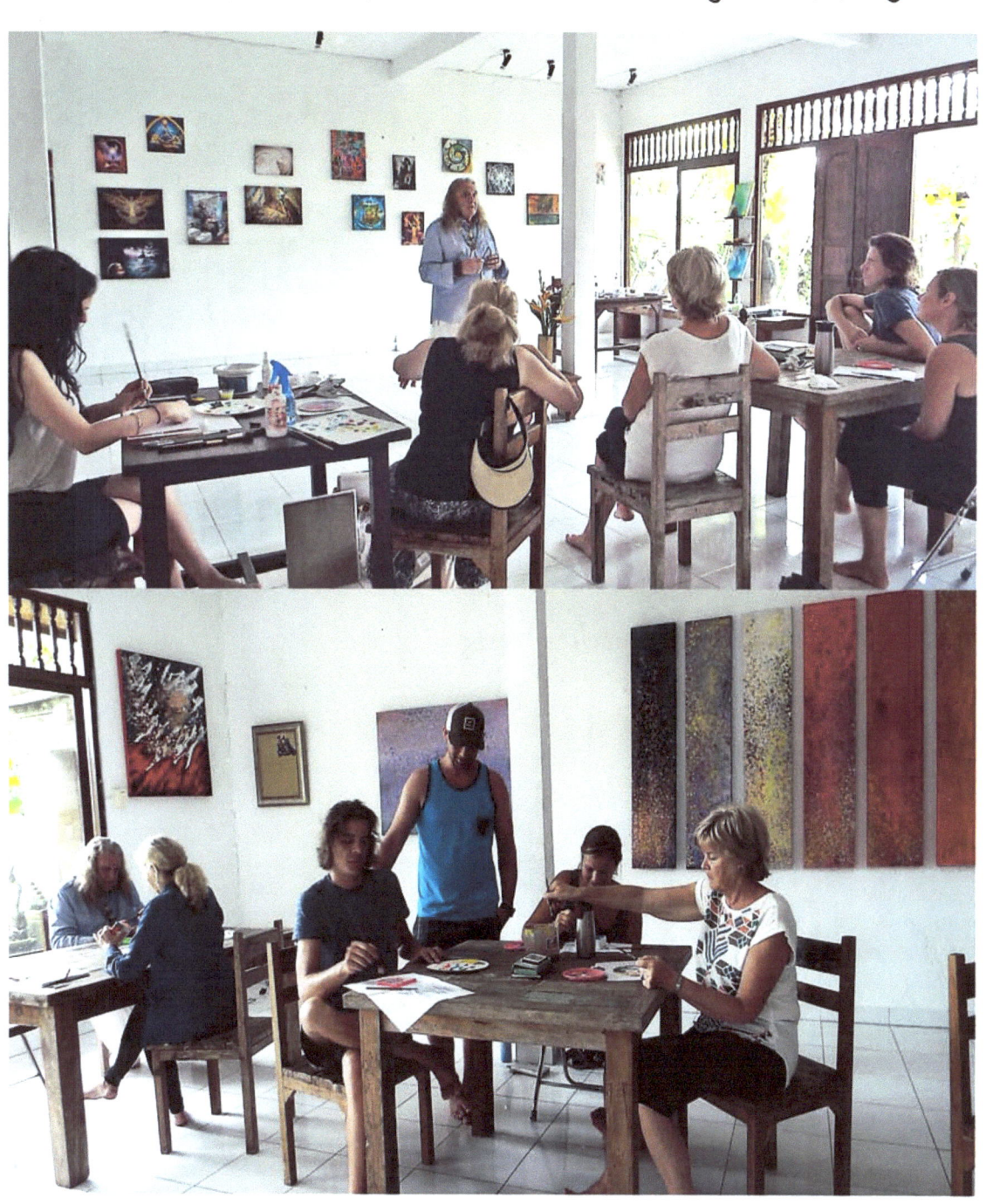

Inspired surrounded by Art & beautiful nature.

Top: Dale, Melissa, Irene, Sylke, Stella, Karina, Robbie & Della Middle: Karina and Stella, Below: Aboetd Art

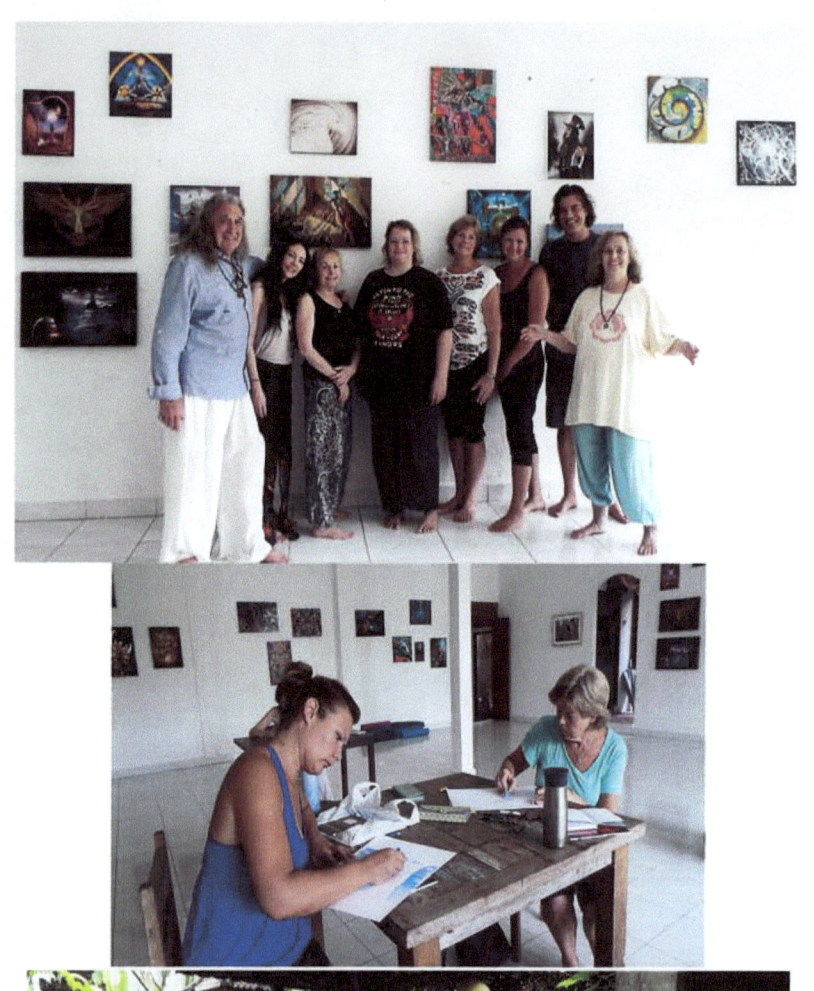
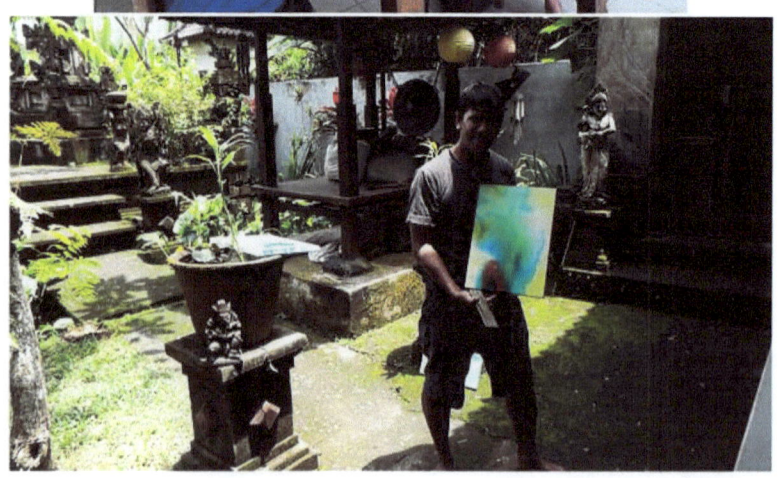

Sylke Gande from Germany
facilitating mini-mandala session & sharing her paintings done at workshops.

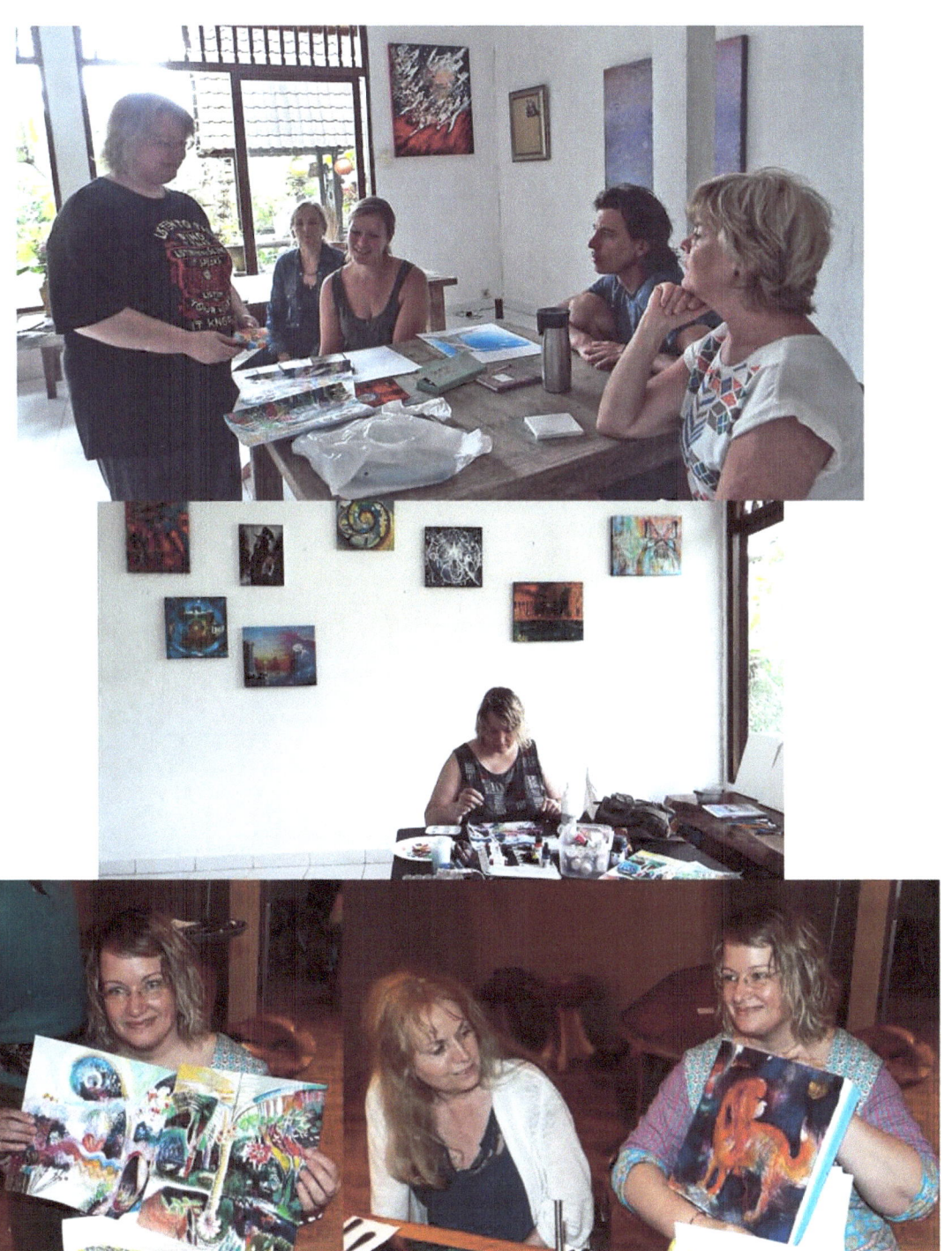

Irene Vincent facilitates a session on the Mische technique.

Irene, Melissa, Della, and Vansi are holding Irene's painting and Brigid Marlins, Below on the table is Cynthia Re Robbins painting also.

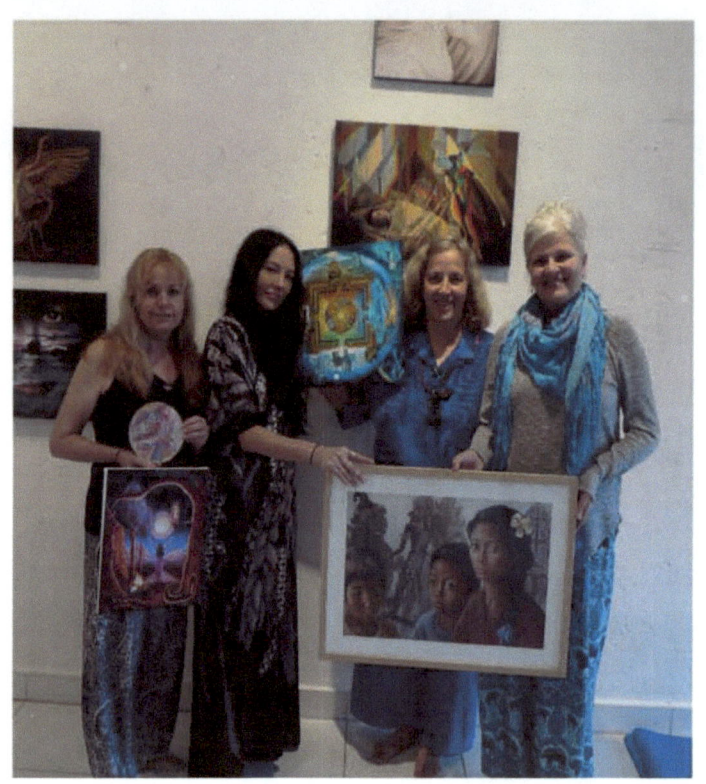

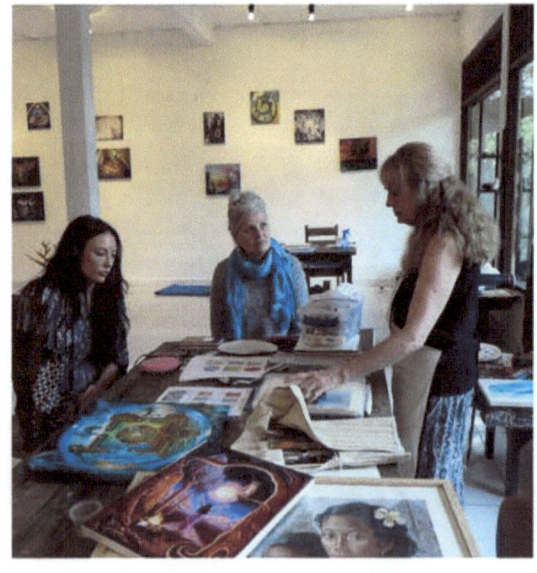

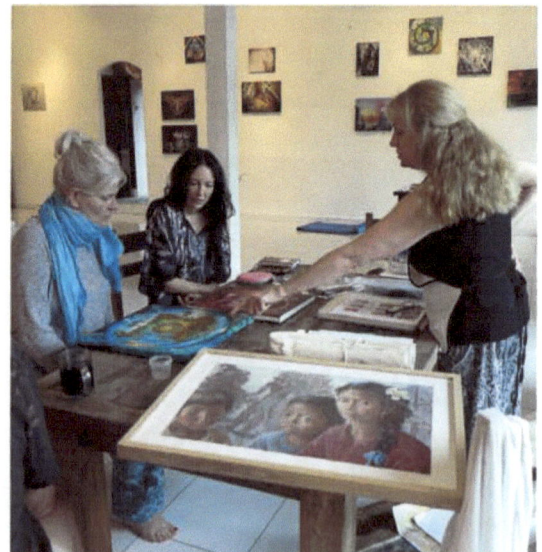

Melissa Fay Marinea & Irene Vincent sharing their art at the Paripurna Dance School.

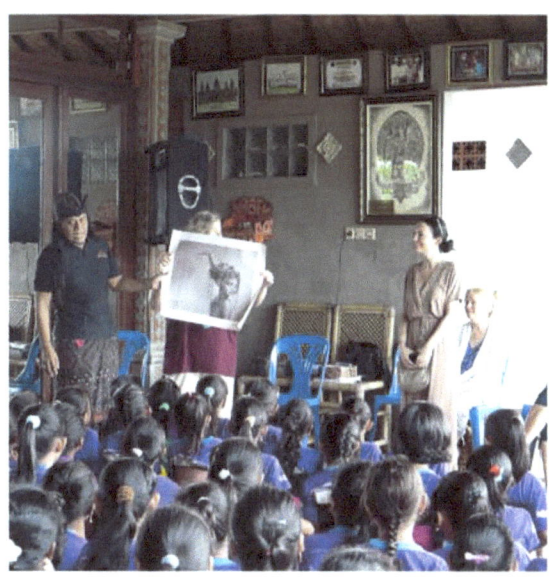

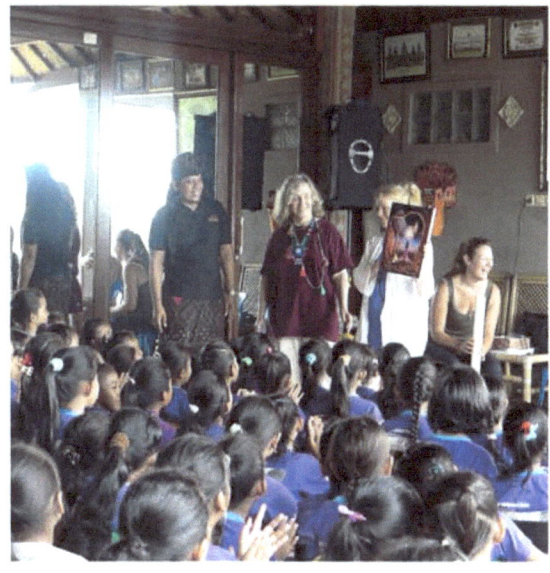

Made Sidia's Dance School
Paripurna danced .. shared life size puppets. Della storytold.

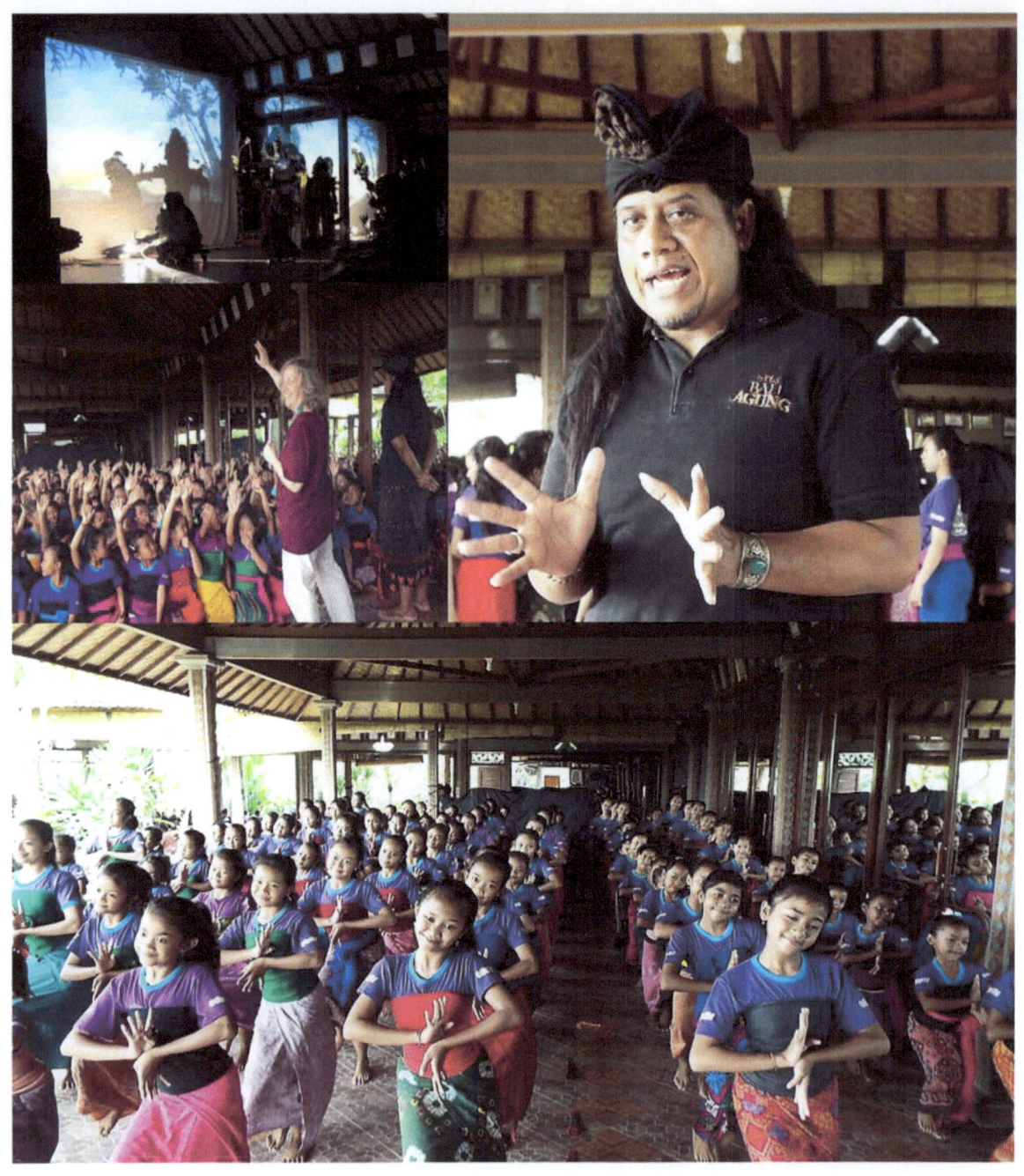

Gusti Lanang and Made Sure helped in getting all the painting ready for the show. Gusti aslo taught a class in Laughter Yoga.

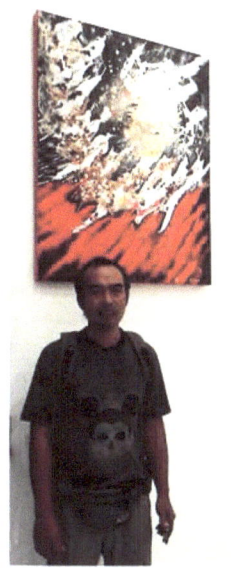
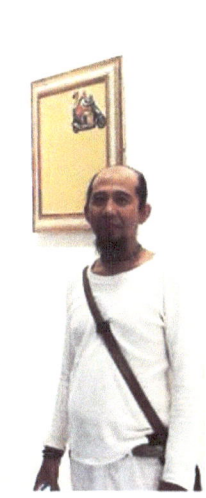
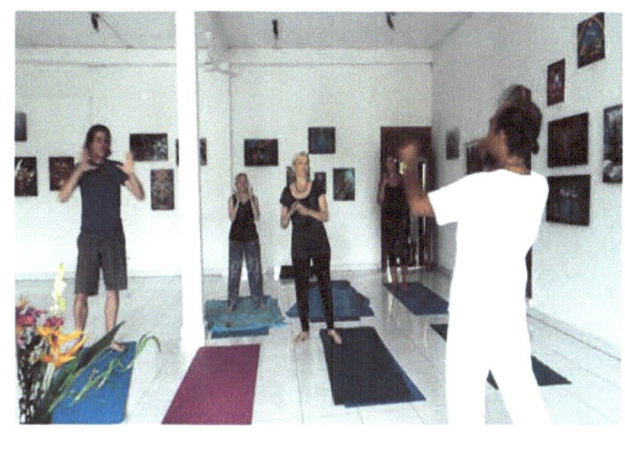
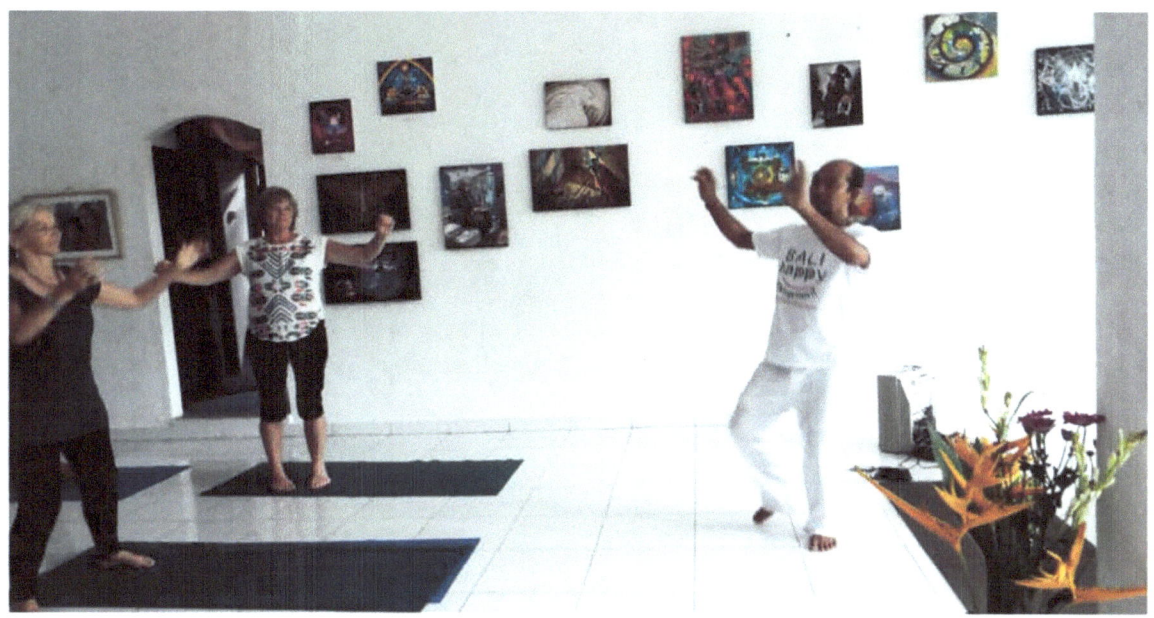

Atman Cafe Nourish – fundraiser for Pelanghi School.

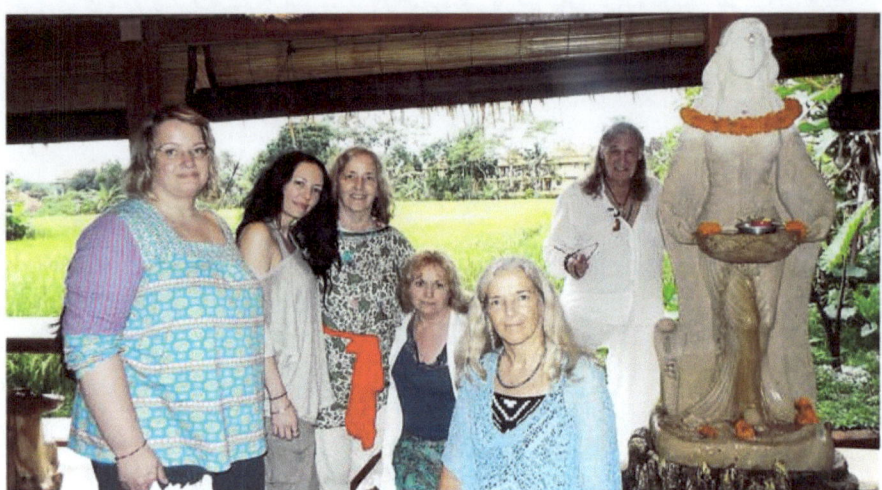

Sylke, Melissa-Fay, Della, Irene, Norah, Dale

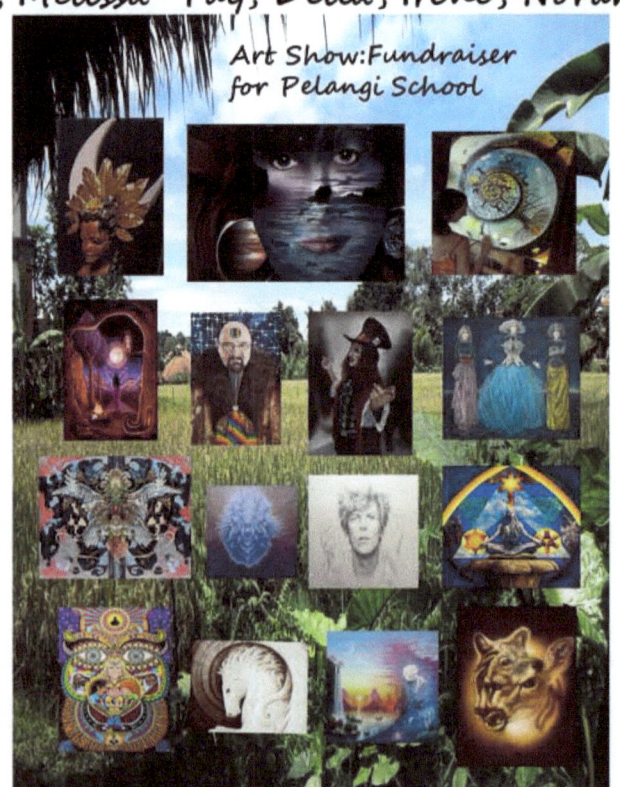

Art Show: Fundraiser for Pelangi School

artist showing: Genevieve, William, Gaia, Irene, Jerome, Debra, Lyne, Heiii, Ricky, Melissa-Fay, Michael, Chris, Andrew, Benny & Duslyn

Brigid Marlin's said she wished for puppets to be at the opening in Bali. As synchronicity has it we were invited by Made Sidia & Paripurna to a life size puppet show being rehearsed for a show in India.

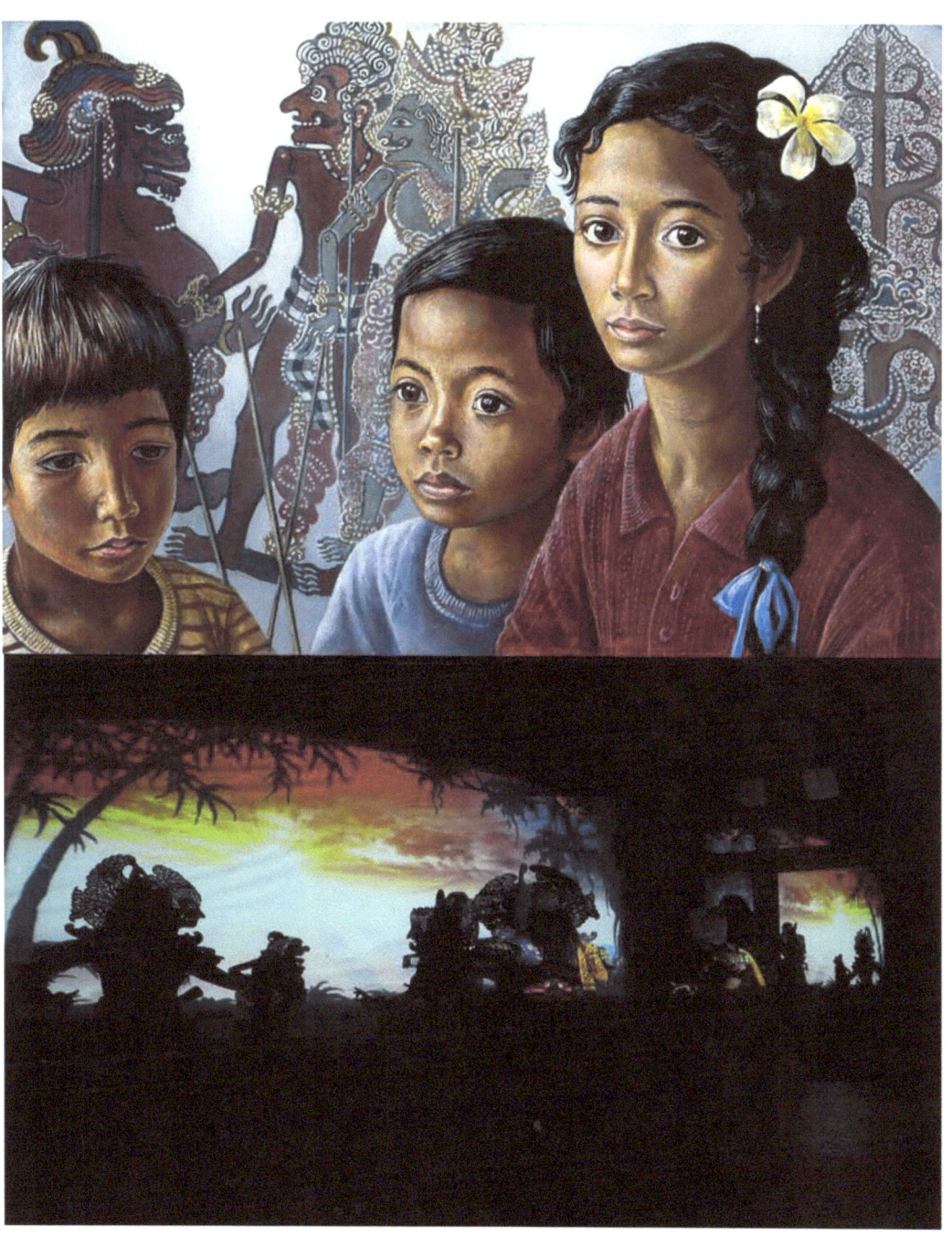

Spirit of Writing and Art
in Bali with Della Burford
Coordinator Norah Burford
co-host Dale Bertrand
Show: Imagination Reigns
with Members of the 'Society
of Art for Imagination'
Jan 26th – Feb 4th 2017
www.spiritofwritingandart.com

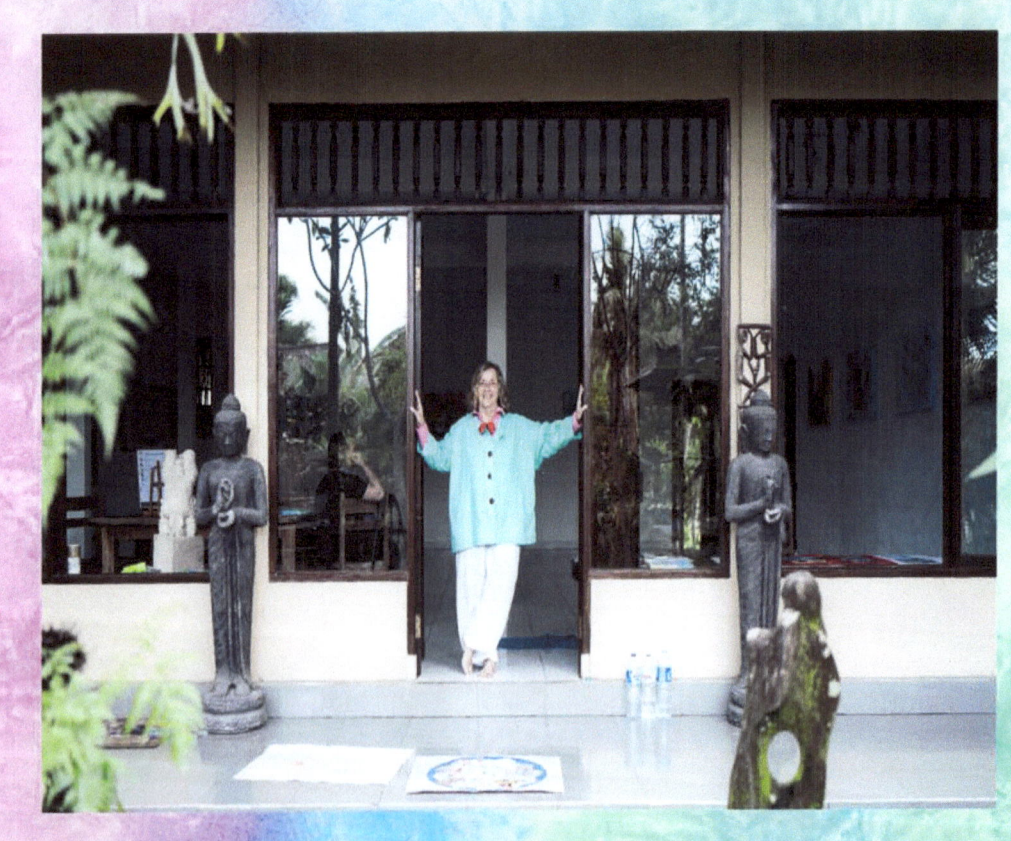

www.ingramcontent.com/pod-product-compliance
Lightning Source LLC
Chambersburg PA
CBHW051212220526
45473CB00003B/1003